Grandma
Traditional Baking

A handbook of useful and practical recipes
for all sorts of baking

Meryl White

AMW Books

Grandma Abson

First published in Great Britain in 2011 by AMW Books

ISBN 978-0-9568703-0-8

Design and artwork by First Class Design Ltd, 01302 515355

Printed and bound by York Publishing Services Ltd.,
64 Hallfield Road, Layerthorpe, York, YO31 7ZQ

Acknowledgements

A huge thank you to all those who have helped me produce
'Grandma Abson's Traditional Recipes'. Thank you to Mark and
colleagues at FCD for combining design flair with meticulous attention
to detail. Also, to Cathi at York Publishing Services for her generous
advice and expertise in taking me through the publishing process.
Finally, I am indebted to my family and friends and in particular
our children, Katherine, Kate and Patrick who have supported
me brilliantly in testing out the recipes, proof reading and offering myriad
suggestions. Enjoy baking with Grandma Abson!

To buy further copies of this book visit: www.ypdbooks.com

Contents

Introduction

Grandma Abson was born Elizabeth (Lizzie) Cave on 21st June 1886 in a two-up two-down terrace in Bolton-on-Dearne, in the West Riding of Yorkshire, to Thomas and Jane Cave. Thomas had come from Rutland to Yorkshire seeking work as a railway platelayer. Lizzie was the second of 10 children (7 girls and 3 boys). Her early years were spent helping her mother to bake and she would talk about kneading 'half a stone' of bread dough before going to school.

On leaving school at the age of 14, Lizzie went into service in nearby Wath-on-Dearne, becoming a 'below

Lizzie outside 6 Station Road in the 1930s

stairs cook' for a local Edwardian business family. "Oakleigh" was the home of the Hick family, a notable family of pharmacists in the district, who frequently entertained prominent local citizens. She stayed there for 10 years. Her philosophy of simple, tasty baking came from these beginnings and she went on to spend a lifetime cooking scrumptious and unpretentious food for her family and friends.

Married in September 1910 to a railway signalman, William Lionel Abson, in a double wedding alongside her elder sister Emma Tooth, she set up home

Lizzie as a young girl in the early 1900s

in a small railway cottage at 6 Station Road, Bolton-on-Dearne. The village, including the railway, had expanded rapidly to accommodate the growth of the mines in the area and brought different jobs to this former farming area. Grandma Abson had two sons but became a widow in 1935. Having lived most of her life in the village, she was well known in the community.

In August 1950, her younger son, Fred, took on the post of Stationmaster at the railway station in Bolton-on-Dearne. His wife, Louisa Doris, had tragically died of leukemia at the young age of 28 in May 1950, leaving behind two small daughters aged 2 months and 4 years, so Grandma came to look after the young family and moved into the Station House. It was a hub of activity in the village, since the railway was well used for travelling around the area and the family was active in village life, largely through its links with the local Methodist Church. Grandma welcomed a constant stream of friends and relatives. Her close friend, Mrs Robson, would pop by every Monday and they would pass the time doing the washing, baking on the cooking range, sharing recipes and talking about what was happening in the village. Mrs Robson was a tall, jolly lady who brought with her a retired police dog called Roger. She was famous for her delicious Date and Walnut Loaf.

Grandma didn't just have her own recipes. She was an avid collector of other people's favourites so, in this edition, I have attributed these where known. Her sisters – Emma Tooth, Alice Page, Clara Cave, Mabel Wood, Edith Sindall and Ivy Henderson were also 'in service', so some of the recipes came from their experiences. Emma did an admirable Plum Pudding. Clara had a penchant for collecting recipes for biscuits. Grandma's repertoire

Lizzie (2nd from left) and her sisters, Emma, Mabel, Alice (4th from left), Edith and Ivy celebrating Alice's Golden Wedding in July 1963.

Grandma Abson with her favourite dog, Flossie in the 1940s

and kept over a longer period, such as the various fruit cakes. Grandma's sisters would write to arrange visits from Manchester and Nottingham and she would always prepare a beautiful spread of afternoon tea, sandwiches and cakes for their arrival, decorating the table with her own embroidered tablecloths. If they arrived at lunchtime, she would cook a traditional British meal of Yorkshire Pudding, beef and vegetables, stews or sausage and mash. She would follow this with one of her scrumptious puddings.

This book is based on Grandma's collection of recipes which she wrote out by hand on scraps of paper and in old exercise books, gathering favourites from relatives and friends, and torn out of magazines. Remembering her biscuits, cakes and puddings from when I was growing up, I began to compile these recipes after my father gave me her old recipe files in 1979. The first edition, entitled 'Grandma Abson's Yorkshire Recipes', produced as a simple booklet in 1981, was a great success. I have produced this revised edition in response to numerous requests and to introduce a wider audience to the delights of home baking. Her recipes cover a wide range of baking, from cakes, biscuits, teabreads and buns to chutneys, jams, tonics and wines. There are old, traditional recipes from her days in service, e.g. St George's Hall Cake, and essentially Yorkshire recipes e.g. Bridlington Cake. She won a prize of 5s (25p) when her Treacle Pudding

was also extended by her daughter-in-law, Nellie Abson (nee Goodwin), with recipes from the Potteries from the 1940s and 50s, including Daffodil Cream and Marmalade Spice Cake. I have my own favourites with Yorkshire Parkin and Simnel Cake at the top of the list. She also got inspiration from magazines such as the 'Woman's Weekly', of which she was a fervent reader.

Visits to the family home were usually unannounced, since there wasn't a telephone in the house until 1963, so Grandma often had to rustle up tea and cakes at short notice. Fortunately, many of her recipes are very quick and simple to prepare or can be made in advance was published in a local newspaper and her Victoria Sponge was a regular prize winner at the local Methodist Chapel summer fairs. Nowadays, the Tonics and Remedies seem quite comical, e.g. Pick Me Up Tonic, though they were all bonafide recipes in their time. I took her Elderberry Syrup and Raspberry Vinegar with me to university to treat coughs and colds in the late 1960s.

Grandma Abson had a stern, rather Victorian outlook on life and a stout work ethic. She lived through some harsh times, raising her family throughout the hardship and rationing of two world wars. Consequently, her recipes were crafted around making tasty food from basic ingredients or limited supplies. Much of Grandma's cooking depended on fresh produce which her husband and later her son (my father) grew in the garden, so her recipes make good use of gluts of fruit and vegetables which are in-season locally. Some lovely examples of this are the chutneys and jams in VII Chutneys, Pickles, Jams and Jellies and her Elderberry Syrup in VIII Wines, Tonics and Remedies, which she made from berries collected in the railway station yard.

The local Methodist Church was an outlet for Grandma Abson's cooking. She regularly baked fruit pies, cakes and biscuits for events like faith teas, where people bring along something to share and take pot luck. She would cook baked potatoes, meat pies followed by blackberry and apple pies for harvest suppers. Everyone wanted a slice of her Apple Pie so they could sample her famous melt in the mouth pastry.

Grandma worked with coal, gas and electric ovens during her life, but she

Bolton-on-Dearne Station: view northward, towards Knottingley and York; ex-Midland & NE Joint (Swinton & Knottingley) main line. Date: 14 September 1962, source: geograph.org.uk, author: Ben Brooksbank

Grandma Abson in the garden at Bolton-on-Dearne Railway station in the 1960s

never was too explicit about cooking times and temperatures. Her early years cooking on black-leaded Yorkshire ranges had given her that mysterious knowledge of what was just the "correct heat". Her reply to the question: "When will it be ready?" was usually, "When it's done"! She did, however, make strict use of a thin cake skewer or cake tester (rather like a thin knitting needle) to stick in the cake and check if it was thoroughly cooked. If it was cooked, there would be no trace of the mixture when the skewer was taken out, but if traces of the mixture remained on the skewer, then it needed further cooking time. I still have her skewer and use it for checking when baking fruit cakes. Oven temperatures were not precise (with slow, moderate and quick as common descriptions) and not always consistent. In this edition, I have included a cooking conversion table for different types of ovens and suggested times and oven temperatures

where these were previously missing. Keep in mind that modern fan ovens should be at a cooler temperature than conventional ovens and may require slightly less cooking time. Neither did Grandma meticulously weigh out the ingredients, hence the many references to "a cupful" or "a basinful", so I have also included a conversion table of metric equivalents for weights and measures.

A lot of Grandma's expertise in baking was based on practice she regarded as common sense, such as making sure the oven was warm and that the ingredients were at room temperature before starting to mix them. She always sieved flour to give a lighter texture. For a fruit cake which needed a lengthy cooking time, she would use copious amounts of newspaper to wrap around the cake tin to prevent burning. She had several wire racks to put her baking on from the oven to allow it to cool. However, she did embrace new technology and was the proud owner of a food mixer and electric whisk by the 1960s.

Grandma Abson died at the grand old age of 91 on 16 December 1977. She had baked her last Christmas cake when she was 90! Her life stretches almost throughout the entire 20th Century but even over this huge period of change and tumult, the recipes remain as fresh and welcome as ever. Grandma Abson began to collect many of her recipes during her time in service, and this book will appeal to all those who are interested in gaining an insight into

One of Grandma Abson's traditional cake and tea spreads, with her crockery from the 1960s.

life 'below stairs'. The book also gives examples of how she baked in times of shortage including wartime rationing. Recipes made without eggs and milk now appeal to those with allergies.

Grandma's recipes tell the story of her love of baking and the collection includes cakes, buns, biscuits and teabreads which are a beautiful combination of simple ingredients from the pantry, classic pudding recipes, and quirky recipes to try out. All form part of her signature baking which made her into such a cherished member of her community. They remind us how quintessentially British it is that people put the kettle on for a cup of tea and a piece of cake and look for a bit of comfort or a treat to deal with all manner of life's difficulties. And isn't it so much better if the cake is lovingly made at home with good ingredients?

The widespread revival of interest in baking has prompted

Grandma's treasure trove of recipes and cooking ideas from 80 years of home baking

me to look again at Grandma's legacy some 30 years after the first edition. This is as much a historical collection as a strict cookery book and I have kept the recipes here as Grandma left them. Grandma Abson's approach combines a no nonsense attitude to baking, the use of good ingredients and the sensuous delight of old fashioned treats. Grandma Abson's recipes are simple, but many of them were created with the idea of making something impressive with basic ingredients.

My family and I regularly bake many of them and it has been great fun reliving the passion I have for home baking and for keeping baking traditions alive. I hope you will take delight in recreating these recipes. Bear in mind that a lot of home baking is often so tempting that it's eaten within 24 hours. Who can resist the joys of a simple fresh sponge cake or the appeal of a tray of biscuits, warm, aromatic and straight out of the oven?

Meryl White

RECIPE INDEX

Conversion tables

Grandma did not use weights, measures and oven temperatures consistently so please see the conversion tables below which you may find useful when following the recipes!

Weights and Measures

oz (ounce)	g (gramme)
1	25
2	50
3	75
4	110
5	150
6	175
7	200
8	225
9	250
10	275
11	300
12	340
13	375
14	400
15	425
16	450

fl oz	ml
1	25
2	50
3	75
4	100-125
5	150
¼ pint/1 gill = 5 fl oz	150
½ pint = 10 fl oz	275-300
1 pint = 20 fl oz	575-600
1 quart = 40 fl oz	1150
1 gallon = 160 fl oz	4600

lb (pound)	g (gramme)
1	450
1½	700
2	900
2½	1100
3	1400

st (stone)	kg (kilo)
1	6.5

Cake tin sizes

7 inch	18 cm
8 inch	21 cm
9 inch	23 cm
10 inch	25 cm

Abbreviations (spoon measures)

1 tbsp	1 tablespoonful (approx 15 ml)
1 dsp	1 dessertspoonful (approx 10 ml)
1 tsp	1 teaspoonful (approx 5 ml)

Oven Temperatures

°F	°C	Gas	Description
250	130	1/2	Very Cool
275	140	1	Very Cool
300	150	2	Cool/slow
325	160-170	3	Warm
350	180	4	Moderate
375	190	5	Fairly Hot/Quick
400	200	6	Fairly Hot
425	210-220	7	Hot
450	230	8	Very Hot
475	240	9	Very Hot

Glossary of Grandma's
baking terminology with helpful hints

Bake it blind	This describes cooking pastry in a dish before putting in the filling. Line the dish with the pastry and then line the pastry with baking paper. Cover this with dried beans or peas. Bake as stated and then remove the paper before putting in the filling. Keep the beans or peas to reuse.
Blend the yeast with the milk	If using fresh or dried yeast, mix the yeast with a liquid before adding to the flour.
Cream the fats and the sugar	Mix the butter and sugar together until the mixture is a pale colour and a fluffy consistency. You can use a wooden spoon, fork or food mixer to do this.
Flour - Plain or self raising?	Self raising flour contains raising agents, usually baking powder, so you don't need to add baking powder. Some recipes give plain flour and baking powder (usually 1 tbsp baking powder to 8oz or 225 g flour). They need sifting well together. For cakes, self raising flour is generally better as it gives a lighter texture. For pastry, plain flour is generally used but Grandma often used ½ plain and ½ self raising to give a softer texture.
Melt the butter in a pan with treacle or golden syrup	Melt the butter over a low heat so that it doesn't burn and add the treacle and golden syrup.
Pastry lid – make a pattern round the edge with a wooden spoon	Once the pastry lid is on the top of a pie, trim the excess pastry off with a knife. Then make a decorative edge. This can be done with a wooden spoon or the edge of a knife to make a fluted, crimped or scalloped edge.
Scald the almonds	Pour boiling water over the almonds to remove the outer skin.
Stew rhubarb in the ordinary way	Cut the rhubarb stem into pieces approximately 2 cms long and then add to a pan with a little water (usually 2-3 tablespoonfuls). Heat the pan and simmer until the rhubarb is soft.

Suggested useful baking items

- Mixing bowls of assorted sizes
- Tins and trays (or silicone moulds) of assorted shapes and sizes : bun, cake, deep, flat, round, sandwich, shallow, square, Yorkshire Pudding
- Wire cooling rack
- Cutters of assorted shapes and sizes
- Pastry brush
- Plastic spatula
- Rolling pin
- Thin, round, metal cake skewer for testing if cakes are cooked
- Palette knife
- Wooden spoons
- Baking paper
- Scales
- Chopping board
- Hand or electric whisk
- Food mixer or processor

Old and new utensils to start baking

I – Cakes
(traditional, plain, sponge, rich)

Grandma's delicious and tempting cakes range from sponge cakes to rich fruit cakes which can be served on seasonal or celebratory occasions, for afternoon tea or simply for enjoyment with family and friends. Sponge cakes, including Almond Cake, Chocolate Cake and Coffee Sandwich were produced when visitors came and were consumed on the same day. She regularly made Orange Cake in a ring tin when she knew someone was coming to tea and she was proud of the fact that she regularly won first prize for her Victoria Sandwich at the local Methodist Church Autumn Fairs.

Unlike the sponge cakes, rich fruit cakes, such as the Christmas Cake recipes, need to be made well before they are required so they can mature. I make my Christmas Cake around late October following her guidance. Other cakes were produced to match the seasons, such as Simnel Cake at Easter or Mothering Sunday and Parkin for Bonfire Night. Grandma regularly made Celebration Cakes for family weddings and this tradition passed down to her niece, Ivy Smallwood, who excelled in cake decorating as well. See the Almond Paste and Sugar Icing in VI Sauces, Icings and Fillings on pages 109 and 110 to complete the decoration.

There are several basic methods of making cakes – 'rubbing in' butter with flour, 'creaming' butter and sugar, 'whisking' eggs with flour and sugar (for fat free sponges) and 'melting' or 'gently heating' sugar, golden syrup, marmalade or honey. Baking cakes is easy, but it really depends on learning about your oven. Things can go wrong if the oven is too hot or too cold. You also need to make sure the mixture is not undercooked or too wet, too dry or unevenly mixed. Grandma learnt how to judge cooking temperatures from experience although I have given guidance by each of the recipes for temperatures in modern fan ovens. A lot of her expertise in baking was based on practice she regarded as common sense, such as making sure the oven was warm and that the ingredients were at room temperature before starting to mix them. She always sieved flour to give a lighter texture. For a fruit cake which needed a lengthy cooking time, she would use copious amounts of newspaper to wrap around the cake tin to prevent burning. Modern ovens often have glass fronts so you can see if the mixture has risen and make an initial judgement without opening the oven door, unlike the coal ranges Grandma cooked on. Grandma did make strict use of a thin cake skewer or cake tester (rather like a thin knitting needle) to stick in the cake and check if it was thoroughly cooked. If it was cooked, there would be no trace of the mixture when the skewer was taken out, but if traces of the mixture remained on the skewer, then it needed further cooking time.

My favourites in this section are the old recipes, such as St George's Hall Cake, School Nut Cake and Wilkins Cake, which are very different from shop bought cakes. The Parkin recipes also feature in my family's top five and hardly ever last to Bonfire night even though they should be left to improve with time. Marmalade Spice Cake and Golden Madeira Cake are more recent additions from the 1950s and these have also become firm favourites. Grandma also had a good selection of basic family fruit loaves and every day cakes such as Cheap Cake, Cherry Cake and Date and Walnut Loaf which always went down well.

——Some common problems with cakes——

Sunk in the middle	– *Mixture is too soft.* – *Oven temperature is too cool so mixture does not rise evenly.* – *Oven temperature is too hot so mixture does not cook evenly.*
Cracking	– *Oven temperature is too hot.* – *Cake is placed too near hottest part of oven.* – *Mixture is too stiff.*
Texture too close	– *Too much liquid is added.* – *Mixture curdles when eggs added (NB add 1 tablespoon of flour to each addition of egg to reduce the risk of curdling).*
Fruit (dried) sunk to the bottom	– *Dried fruit is too damp.* – *Glacé cherries are sticky (NB always wash and dry glacé cherries before use).*

Paradise Cake

Dream Cake

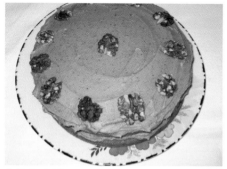

Coffee Sandwich

Chocolate Cake

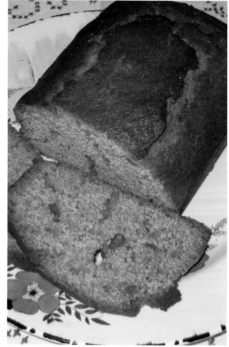

Marmalade Spice Cake

Un-cooked Marmalade Spice Cake

Contents
Cakes (traditional, plain, sponge, rich)

ALMOND CAKE
Very Good Recipe

This is a light textured cake which has a strong flavour of almonds.

4 oz butter

4 oz caster sugar

2 eggs (beaten)

2 oz ground almonds

5 oz self raising flour

Almond essence – few drops

Spot of milk

Pinch of salt

"Grease and line a 7 inch cake tin. Cream the butter, sugar and almond essence. Add the eggs gradually. Mix the flour, ground almonds and salt, and add to the creamed mixture. Add enough milk to give a soft consistency. Bake in a warm oven for 1 hour." (325°F, Mark 3, 170°C)

GERMAN ALMOND CAKE
Clara Cave

Grandma's younger sister, Clara, had her own version of Almond Cake from when she was in service in Didsbury, Manchester in the 1920s and 30s. The recipe is of German origin. Grandma used to stir the egg yolk and sugar mixture for half an hour but these days you can save time by using an electric whisk on a slow setting for 2 to 3 minutes. Use ground almonds where Clara suggests 'sweet' almonds.

1 lb sweet almonds

1 lb caster sugar

12 eggs

4 dsps plain flour

"The yolk of the eggs must be stirred with the sugar for ½ hour, or mixed with an electric whisk on a slow setting for 2 to 3 minutes. Then add the almonds, the flour and the whites of eggs beaten to a froth. Put the mixture at once in a tin and let it bake for 1¼ hours in a slow oven. This quantity is for a medium sized cake, a half of everything may be taken for a smaller one." (300°F, Mark 2, 150°C)

CELEBRATION CAKES:

BOXING DAY CAKE

This is a special cake for Boxing Day which has an unusual hint of almond and honey giving it a taste of North Africa.

6 oz margarine or butter
and lard (mixed)

1 tbsp sugar

3 tbsps honey

3 eggs

4 oz dates

1/4 tsp grated nutmeg

Pinch of salt

Few drops of almond essence

1 lb self raising flour (sifted)

Milk to mix

"Cream the fats, sugar and honey. Slowly beat in the eggs. Then add the dates (cut into quarters), nutmeg, salt and almond essence. Gradually, fold in the sifted flour. Beat well with a wooden spoon. Add a little milk. Put into a greased and lined 8 inch tin. Bake in a slow oven for about 1 hour." (300°F, Mark 2, 150°C)

BRIDE'S CAKE

This provides sufficient mixture for two cake tins such as the two horseshoe cakes which Grandma made for her elder granddaughter's wedding. Use ground almonds for sweet almonds.

3/4 lb butter

3/4 lb sugar

6 eggs

1/4 lb golden syrup (slightly warmed)

1/2 pt milk (slightly warmed) or a little stout made up to 1/2 pt with milk

3 lb currants/sultanas/raisins mixed

1/4 lb glace cherries

1/4 lb lemon peel

1/4 lb sweet almonds

1 lb self raising flour

A little brandy

"Work the butter to a cream and add the sugar. Drop in the eggs one by one. Beat well. Then add the golden syrup and milk. Add the flour, fruit and nuts. Finally, add the brandy. Bake in a moderate oven for 4½ - 5 hours gradually reducing the temperature." (300°F, Mark 2, 150°C)

CHRISTMAS CAKE
Oakleigh - Very Good Old Recipe

This is a very old Christmas Cake recipe which Grandma would have used in service at 'Oakleigh' as it makes four small cakes to consume over the Christmas period. Clearly, if you only need one cake, you can divide each of the quantities by four. All the Christmas Cakes would have been made well in advance in late October or early November.

2 lb flour

1 lb sugar

1 lb butter or margarine

1 lb stoned raisins (chopped)

1½ lb sultanas

1½ lb currants

½ lb mixed peel or rind of orange and lemon

1 tsp salt

½ tsp baking powder

1 tbsp dark treacle

Nutmeg and spice to taste

8 eggs

A little milk

"Follow Bride's Cake for method and temperature."

CHRISTMAS CAKE
written as Grandma made in 1971

Grandma had adapted her Christmas Cake recipes by the early 1970s, using self raising flour and adding brandy once the cake was cool to keep it moist. She used to wrap several layers of brown paper or newspaper around the tin and tie it with string to prevent burning before putting the cake into the oven.

1½ lb butter

1 lb soft brown sugar

¼ lb cane sugar

10 eggs

1½ lb self raising flour

½ lb ground almonds or almond nibs

1 pkt nut mix or chopped nuts

¼ lb mixed peel

¼ lb glace cherries (chopped)

2½ lb currants

2 lb sultanas

1 tbsp black treacle

¼ lb warmed golden syrup

½ bottle of stout

1 tsp grated nutmeg or mixed spice

A pinch of salt

A little brandy

"Grease and line a 9 inch cake tin. Cream the butter and sugar. Add the eggs gradually. Add the treacle and golden syrup. Mix together the flour, salt, chopped nuts, ground almonds, nutmeg or mixed spice and fruit and

add to the creamed mixture. Add a little stout. Bake in a slow oven for 4 - 4½ hours (300°F, Mark 2, 150°C), gradually reducing to very slow oven (250°F, Mark 1, 130°C). Test the cake with a skewer until it comes out clean. Leave to cool then prick with a fine skewer and slowly pour a little brandy over it. Wrap in greaseproof paper and place in an airtight tin. Store in a cool place."

CHRISTMAS CAKE - 8 inch

This is a foolproof recipe I have used for many years every Christmas. There is rarely a piece of it left by 1 January!

8 oz brown sugar

8 oz butter

1 tbsp black treacle (warmed)

1 tbsp golden syrup (warmed)

5 eggs (beaten)

9 oz self raising flour

3-4 oz glace cherries

4 oz mixed peel

10 oz each of sultanas, raisins, currants

1tsp each of cinnamon and mixed spice

2oz nut mix + 1oz ground almonds or 3oz ground almonds

⅙ pint stout

"Cream the butter and sugar and add the treacle and golden syrup. Add the eggs and half of the flour and spices. Beat the mixture. Stir in the almonds and cherries and then the rest of the flour and dried fruit. Add the stout. Bake for 3 – 3 ½ hours. Start warm for 30 minutes and then gradually reduce and finish in slow oven." (325°F, Mark 3, 170°C to 250°F, Mark ½, 130°C)

YULE CAKE

An alternative to Christmas cake which is made in the same way as making bread.

2 lb plain flour

1 lb currants

1 lb sugar

½ lb sultanas

½ lb lard

2 oz peel

1 pint milk

2 eggs

3 oz yeast

½ tsp bicarbonate of soda

"Rub the flour and lard together. Add the sugar, fruit and peel. Beat the eggs and add to the mixture. Dissolve the bicarbonate of soda in a cup of milk. Mix the yeast in the rest of the warm milk with a spoon. Add to the other mixture. Let it rise in a bowl for ½ hour. Put into tins. Leave another ½ hour to rise in a warm place. Bake in a moderate oven for 2 – 2½ hours." (350°F, Mark 4, 180°C)

BRIDLINGTON CAKE

This cake takes its name from the railway excursions to Bridlington on the Yorkshire coast. Grandma used to have this cake prepared for the trips to the coast or for the arrival home. The cake has a summery lemon flavour.

1/2 lb butter

1/2 lb sugar

4 eggs

Grated rind of one lemon

1/2 lb cornflour

1/2 tsp baking powder

"Beat the butter to a cream and add the sugar, grated lemon rind and yolks of eggs (well beaten). Beat the whites of eggs until stiff and then add the flour, stirring the mixture as lightly as possible. Finally, add the baking powder. Bake in a slow oven for about 1 hour." (300°F, Mark 2, 150°C)

CHEAP CAKE

'Cheap' in this context means less 'rich' than the richness of the fruit cakes for wedding and festive celebrations but it is still a tasty cake.

1/2 lb butter

1/2 lb sugar

4 eggs (beaten)

1 cup of milk

1 lb plain flour

1/2 oz baking powder

Currants and peel as you like

"Cream the butter and sugar. Add the eggs and milk. Fold in the flour and baking powder. Add currants and peel as you like. Bake in a moderate oven for 1 hour." (350°F, Mark 4, 180°C)

CHERRY CAKE

The trick with this recipe is to wash and dry the cherries before adding to the mixture so they don't fall to the bottom of the cake.

¹/₂ lb butter

¹/₂ lb caster sugar

¹/₂ lb self raising flour

4 small eggs

6 oz glace cherries

A little grated lemon rind

"Beat the butter and sugar to a cream, add each egg separately and beat in well. The mixture must be kept stiff. Sift in the flour and stir into the creamed mixture. Lastly, add the cherries (cut into small pieces), and the lemon rind. Put into a tin lined with greased paper and bake for 1-1¹/₂ hours in a warm oven." (325°F, Mark 3, 160-170°C)

CHOCOLATE CAKE

This is a simpler version of a Chocolate Cake which can be decorated with a dusting of icing sugar or cocoa powder. It's one of my favourites since it's quick to make and light in texture.

6 oz margarine or butter

6 oz sugar

6 oz self raising flour

2 tbsps cocoa

A pinch of salt

3 eggs

2 tbsps treacle (warmed)

¹/₂ tsp vanilla essence

¹/₂ cup milk

"Cream the margarine (or butter) and sugar. Mix the cocoa and flour together with a pinch of salt. Beat the eggs. Add alternately to the mixture with the flour. Add the treacle and vanilla to taste. Add a little milk to give a soft consistency. Bake in a moderate oven for ³/₄ hour." (350°F, Mark 4, 180°C)

CHOCOLATE LAYER CAKE

This is a more modern recipe which Grandma made in the early 1960s as chocolate became more readily available. It has a stunning mocha taste with the combination of coffee and chocolate in the filling. This recipe reflects the cooking trends of the time by being more complex and including more ingredients. For the filling, the granules of coffee need to be crushed to a powder first.

4 oz butter or margarine

4 oz sugar

2 large eggs

2 tbsps cocoa

1½ tbsps hot water

4 oz self raising flour

"Cream the butter and sugar and add well beaten eggs. Blend the cocoa with the water and beat into the mixture. Fold in the flour. Bake in a moderate oven for 25 minutes." (375°F, Mark 5, 190°C)

Filling

3 oz caster sugar

Pinch of cream of tartar

3 tbsps water

2 small or 1 large egg yolk(s)

4 oz butter

2 oz plain chocolate (melted)

2 level tsps instant coffee powder

"Put the sugar and cream of tartar in a small pan. Add the water and dissolve the sugar over a low heat. Bring to the boil. Cool slightly whilst beating the egg yolk(s). Pour the liquid from the pan into the yolk(s). Cream the butter and pour on the syrup mixture, beating all the time. Beat in the melted chocolate and instant coffee powder. Continue to beat until the mixture is thick enough to spread. Split the cake and insert the filling."

Icing

Cover the top with Chocolate Glace Icing as follows:-

1 oz grated chocolate

1½ tbsp water

2½ oz icing sugar

"Place the chocolate and water in a pan and stir until the chocolate is melted. Remove from heat and stir in sufficient icing sugar to give a coating consistency."

COFFEE SANDWICH

A simple coffee cake which is easy to make. The walnuts give it an elegant touch. If you use coffee granules, make sure you grind them first to a powder, for example, in a pestle and mortar.

4 oz sugar

6 oz self raising flour

4 oz margarine or butter

3 eggs

1 small tsp baking powder

1 dsp coffee essence or powder

"Cream the butter and sugar, add the coffee essence or powder. Mix well. Add the flour and eggs alternately. And lastly, add the baking powder. Divide into 2 sandwich tins and bake in a moderate oven for 30 minutes or more." (350°F, Mark 4, 180°C)

Filling:

"Cream 1½ oz margarine or butter and 3 oz sugar. Add a little milk, beat well and add 1 dessertspoonful coffee essence. Decorate with walnuts."

DATE AND WALNUT LOAF

Mrs. Robson

Mrs Robson was one of Grandma's close friends. The combination of date and walnuts gives a slightly crunchy flavour to the loaf. This was her signature recipe.

1 lb dates (chopped)

1 cup boiling water

2 oz margarine or butter

1 cup sugar

1 egg

2 cups plain flour

1 tsp bicarbonate of soda

½ tsp cinnamon

½ tsp cloves

2 oz shelled walnuts

"Cover the dates with the boiling water and leave until cool. Cream the margarine (or butter) and sugar. Add the egg (well beaten) and other ingredients (flour, bicarbonate of soda, cinnamon, cloves and walnuts). Finally, drain the dates and add to the mixture. Put in a bread tin (well greased). Leave to stand for 20 minutes. Bake in a slow oven for 1 hour." (300°F, Mark 2, 150°C)

DUTCH APPLE CAKE

There is a noted Dutch influence in Yorkshire cooking since Dutch engineers came across to build the dykes to drain the flood water from the fields in the Vale of York and on the banks of the Humber. A Dutch friend says she remembers her Grandma making something like this. The apples give this cake a moist texture. This cake will keep only a few days but you will find it is so tasty it soon disappears! It could also be classed as a pudding and served with custard or ice cream.

8 oz plain flour

$^1/_2$ tsp baking powder

2 oz sugar

$2^1/_2$ oz margarine or butter

Pinch of salt

1 egg

3 tbsps milk

A little nutmeg

2 large or 3 medium apples

For top:

3 oz sugar

$^1/_2$ tsp cinnamon

"Sift the baking powder with the flour. Cut the margarine or butter into pieces into the flour, add the rest of the dry ingredients and add the milk and beaten egg gradually. Mix to a fairly soft dough, turn on to a lightly floured board and roll out to line an 8 inch cake tin (square and about $1^1/_2$ inches deep). Peel, core and cut the apples into $^1/_2$ inch slices, press the sharp edges of the apples into the dough closely together and sprinkle the sugar and cinnamon over the top. Bake in a quick oven for 1 hour, on the top shelf for the first 15 minutes." (375°F, Mark 5, 190°C)

DREAM CAKE

The reason for the name of this cake is lost in the mists of time – but it's a dream if you like cherries and walnuts. Don't forget to wash and dry the cherries before you add them to the mixture.

5 oz margarine or butter

5 oz sugar

Vanilla essence

3 eggs

8 oz self raising flour

1 level tsp baking powder

3 oz cherries

3 oz walnuts

"Line a cake tin. Cream the margarine or butter and sugar. Beat the eggs thoroughly. Add the vanilla essence. Add a little flour and the eggs alternately, adding baking powder last of all. Fold in the walnuts and cherries, which have been rolled in flour, saving a few for the top of the cake. Bake in a moderate oven for about 1 hour."
(350°F, Mark 4, 180°C)

FAMILY FRUIT CAKES:

FRUIT CAKE WITHOUT EGGS
Oakleigh

Grandma was in service at Oakleigh, a large Victorian house in Wath-on-Dearne. This cake is good for those who cannot or prefer not to eat eggs, a precursor to recipes by modern bakers who now produce ranges for those with allergies to eggs.

½ lb sugar

6 oz butter

½ lb plain flour

½ lb ground rice flour

6 oz currants

6 oz sultanas

2 oz mixed peel

Nutmeg and spice to taste

½ pint milk

1 tsp bicarbonate of soda

"Cream the butter and sugar well. Sift in the flour and all dry ingredients. Heat the milk and dissolve the bicarbonate of soda in it. Mix well. Bake 1½ - 2 hours in a slow oven." (300°F, Mark 2, 150°C)
"To make a richer cake, add ½ lb currants and ½ lb sultanas."

FRUIT CAKE WITHOUT EGGS OR MILK

This fruit cake is an alternative to the previous recipe which is perfect for those with allergies to eggs and milk.

3 oz sugar

3 oz margarine or butter

6 oz dried fruit

1½ gills of water

9 oz plain flour

1½ tsp bicarbonate of soda

2 level tsps ground cinnamon

½ level tsp ground cloves or mixed spice

"Put sugar, fat, fruit and water into a pan. Heat these ingredients slowly until they are dissolved. Then boil gently for 3 or 4 minutes. Leave this mixture until it is almost cold, but not set. Then sift the flour, spices and soda into a basin. Stir in the boiled mixture when cold enough. Put into a greased tin and bake in a warm oven for 1-1½ hours." (325°F, Mark 3, 170°C) "Let it stand in tin after taking from oven."

FRUIT AND NUT CAKE

This is a good alternative to Date and Walnut Loaf.

10 oz plain flour

2 tsps baking powder

4 oz butter

4 oz sugar

4 oz sultanas

4 oz walnuts

4 oz ground almonds

A little milk

2 eggs (beaten)

"Mix the flour and baking powder. Rub the butter into the flour until the mixture resembles breadcrumbs. Stir in the sugar, sultanas, walnuts and ground almonds. Add the eggs and a little milk to give a soft consistency. Bake in a moderate oven 1-1¼ hours." (350°F, Mark 4, 180°C)

GENOA CAKE

The lemon rind gives this fruity cake a hint of the Mediterranean, from which this cake derives its name.

6 oz butter or margarine

6 oz caster sugar

4 eggs (beaten)

8 oz plain flour

Grated rind of one lemon

4 oz sultanas

3 oz glace cherries

5 oz currants

4 oz chopped peel

1 tbsp milk

"Cream the butter and sugar. Add the eggs gradually. Mix the flour, lemon rind and fruit. Add to the creamed mixture. Add the milk. Bake for 2 - 2½ hours in a warm oven."
(325°F, Mark 3, 170°C)

OVERNIGHT CAKE

This cake is exactly as its name says – you leave it overnight before cooking. It keeps well in an airtight tin.

1 lb plain flour

½ lb margarine or lard

½ tsp nutmeg

½ tsp mixed spice

½ lb sugar

2 tsps bicarbonate of soda

1 lb mixed dried fruit

2 eggs (beaten)

1 pint milk (or milk and water)

"Rub the margarine into the flour and add the other dried ingredients. Mix in the eggs and milk. Leave in a bowl overnight. Place the mixture in a 9 inch tin. Bake in a slow oven for 1½ - 2 hours."
(300°F, Mark 2, 150°C)

PARADISE CAKE

Grandma loved coming up with bizarre names for her cakes. Paradise Cake is a fruity cake which is slightly lighter than some of the previous fruit cakes in this section.

9 oz plain flour

6 oz margarine or butter

6 oz sugar

2 oz nuts

8 oz raisins

2 oz mixed peel

2 oz cherries

3 eggs

Lemon essence

½ tsp baking powder

"Sieve the flour and baking powder. Beat the margarine or butter and sugar until white. Beat the eggs lightly and add to the mixture. Mix well and add the flour gradually, keeping out a little in which to mix the fruit and nuts. Add this and lastly the lemon essence and baking powder. Bake for 1 - 1½ hours in a moderate oven." (350°F, Mark 4, 180°C)

POUND CAKE

as made at Oakleigh in 1912

This is an easy to remember recipe as for most of the ingredients you just need one pound in weight (450 g). It keeps well. The recipe comes from Grandma's days in service at the house called Oakleigh.

1 lb butter

1 lb sugar

8 eggs (beaten)

1 lb plain flour

1 tsp baking powder

2 lb currants (or 1 lb currants, 1 lb raisins or sultanas)

½ lb finely cut peel

A few chopped almonds

Pinch of nutmeg, cinnamon and mace

Small wineglass of brandy if preferred or milk to mix

"Grease and line a 9 inch cake tin. Cream the butter and sugar. Add the eggs gradually. Mix the flour, baking powder, fruit, almonds and spices. Add these to the creamed mixture. Add the brandy or milk to give a soft consistency. Bake in a slow oven for 3 hours." (300°F, Mark 2, 150°C)

RICH CAKE

This is a good fruit cake recipe which is a treat all year round because of its richer texture from adding warm golden syrup.

¼ lb butter

¼ lb sugar

6 eggs (beaten)

¼ lb syrup (warm)

½ pt milk

1 lb self raising flour

¼ lb glace cherries

¼ lb mixed peel

3 lbs fruit (mixed sultanas, currants, raisins)

A little stout

"Grease and line a 9 inch cake tin. Cream the butter and sugar. Add the eggs gradually. Add the syrup and milk. Mix together the flour and fruit and add to the creamed mixture. Add a little stout. Bake in a slow oven for 3 hours." (300°F, Mark 2, 150°C)

SCHOOL NUT CAKE
Very Good Recipe

Another old recipe from Grandma's days in service which she had noted was a very good one. 'School' cakes were so-called as they were generally classed as plainer and for everyday use. They were especially suitable for children.

2 cups plain flour

½ tsp baking powder

1 cup sugar

½ cup raisins

½ cup chopped walnuts

1 tsp salt

1 egg (beaten)

1 cup milk

"Grease and line a 7 inch cake tin. Mix together flour, baking powder, sugar, raisins, walnuts and salt. Add the egg and then the milk. Let it stand for ½ hour. Bake in a warm oven for 1 hour." (325°F, Mark 3, 170°C)

SCRIPTURE CAKE

This recipe is humorously titled 'Scripture Cake' as all the ingredients have references from the Old Testament.

4½ cupfuls of 1st Kings iv 22
= 4½ cups of plain flour

1½ cupfuls of Judges v 25
= 1½ cups of butter

2 cupfuls of Jeremiah vi 20
= 2 cups of sugar

2 cupfuls of 1st Samuel xxx 12
= 2 cups of raisins

2 cupfuls of Nahum iii 12
= 2 cups of figs

1 cupful of Numbers xvii 8
= 1 cup of almonds

2 tablespoonfuls of 1st Samuel xiv 25
= 2 tbsps of honey

6 Jeremiah xvii 11
= 6 eggs

A Pinch of Leviticus ii 13
= A pinch of salt

Season with 2nd Chronicles ix 9
= Season to taste with spices

½ cup Judges iv 19
= ½ cup of milk

2 teaspoonfuls of Amos iv 5
= 2 tsps of yeast

"Beat all together and bake in a moderate oven for 2½ hours."
(350°F, Mark 4, 180°C)

SLAB CAKE

You can cut this fruit cake into squares rather than slices – hence its name.

8 oz butter

8 oz sugar

5 eggs (beaten)

10 oz plain flour

2 tsps baking powder

4 oz ground almonds

8 oz sultanas

4 oz glace cherries

4 oz walnuts

"Grease and line a 9 inch square cake tin. Cream the butter and sugar. Add the eggs gradually. Mix together the flour, baking powder, ground almonds, fruit and walnuts. Add these to the creamed mixture. Bake in a slow oven for 2 - 2½ hours."
(300°F, Mark 2, 150°C)

SPICE CAKE

The mixed spice gives this cake a real tangy flavour. Make this in summer to have with a glass of fizz or in winter with hot chocolate, punch or mulled wine.

4 oz butter

6 oz lard

8 oz sugar

3 eggs (beaten)

¼ lb plain flour

¼ lb ground rice flour

1 tsp baking powder

1 tsp mixed spice

8 oz currants

8 oz sultanas

4 oz candied peel

Pinch of salt

A little milk to mix

"Grease and line an 8 inch cake tin. Cream the butter and fat with the sugar. Add the eggs gradually. Mix the flours, baking powder, mixed spice, salt and dried fruit together. Fold these into the creamed mixture. Add a little milk to give a soft consistency. Bake in a slow oven for 2½ - 3 hours." (300°F, Mark 2, 150°C) "The same recipe can be used for **'Seed Cake'** omitting the fruit and adding 3 tsps caraway seed and 1 tbsp ground almonds."

ST. GEORGE'S HALL CAKE
Oakleigh

A recipe from Oakleigh where Grandma was in service. This is one of the first ones I tried out when I collated the recipes. The currants give it quite a different feel from modern cakes. A great cake for St George's Day!

¼ lb butter

¼ lb sugar

2 eggs

½ lb plain flour

1 tsp baking powder

A little salt

¼ lb currants

2 oz candied peel

½ cupful milk

"Work the butter to a cream. Add the sugar and beat well together. Add the eggs (well beaten), flour, baking powder, salt, currants, candied peel and milk. Beat well for 5 minutes. Bake in a warm oven for 1¼ - 1½ hours." (325°F, Mark 3, 170°C) "This is sufficient to make one cake only. Double the quantity to make two. This recipe makes a very nice plain cake with currants omitted."

Making a Christmas Cake *(see recipes on page 22)*

Wrap the cake tin with newspaper before it goes in the oven

Let the cake cool before removing from the tin

Let your imagination run wild or keep it simple with traditional decorations

All set for afternoon tea with Grandma's cake stand. Put the kettle on and enjoy a Yorkshire treat of
Coffee Sandwich (page 27), Fruit Harvo (page 62), Sweet Biscuits (page 77) and Coconut Fingers (page 71)

SULTANA CAKE
Excellent Old Recipe

Grandma clearly thought this was the 'top of the cakes' since she gave this high praise indeed when she noted it as an excellent old recipe – it's simple and keeps well.
You need a small pot or glass basin to measure the ingredients.

½ lb lard or butter (8oz)

1 basin sugar (6oz)

4 eggs (beaten)

1½ basins plain flour (8oz)

¾ basin ground rice (4oz)

8 tsps baking powder

1 basin sultanas (6oz)

¼ lb candid peel (4oz)

Pinch salt

Pinch nutmeg

"Grease and line an 8 inch cake tin. Cream the fat and the sugar. Beat the eggs and add gradually to the mixture. Mix together the flour, baking powder, ground rice, salt, nutmeg and fruit. Add these to the creamed mixture. Bake in a warm oven for 1½ - 2 hours."
(325°F, Mark 3, 170°C)

WILKINS CAKE

I love the idea of a cup of this and a cup of that which takes away the problem of metric translations. I never found out who Wilkins was – but Grandma's husband was William Lionel so maybe it was his favourite.

3 oz margarine or butter

1 cup sugar

2 cups plain flour

1 tsp baking powder

1 cup raisins

1 cup water

1 tsp cinnamon

1 tsp ginger

¼ grated nutmeg

Pinch salt

"Melt the margarine in a pan. Boil the sugar in water for 3 minutes. When cold, add the flour and the baking powder. Add the spices, salt and raisins. Mix well. Bake for 1 - 1¼ hours in a warm oven."
(300°F, Mark 3, 150°C)

FAMILY FRUIT LOAVES:

FAMILY FRUIT LOAF

Fruit loaf is a great classic staple to accompany afternoon tea.

2 lbs self raising flour

½ lb margarine or butter

½ lb sugar

½ lb currants

½ lb raisins

1 nutmeg (grated)

3 eggs

1 pint milk

"Rub the fat into the flour. Add all of the dry ingredients. Whisk the eggs with the milk and mix all together well. Bake for 1 hour in a moderate oven in 2 x 1 lb loaf tins." (350°F, Mark 4, 180°C)

FRUIT LOAF

Since this recipe is based on a cup of this and a cup of that, you can make this recipe without owning a set of kitchen scales – you just need a cup! It is up to you how big a cup you use. I would advise you use a tea cup to create a cake with roughly eight slices.

3 cups self raising flour

½ cup sugar

1 cup of sultanas

1 tsp salt

2 eggs

1½ cups milk

"Mix together all of the dried ingredients. Add the eggs and milk, and beat thoroughly. Put into a well greased tin. Allow to rise for 2 hours. Bake in a moderate oven for 1¼ hours." (350°F, Mark 4, 180°C)

Stages in making Scones *(see recipe on page 65)*

Assemble the ingredients

Roll out the dough

Cut out the scones

Serve with butter or cream and jam

GINGER CAKE

We love the tangy taste of Ginger Cake which makes this recipe a real favourite in our family. It also keeps well and retains its moisture.

4 oz butter

8 oz treacle

3 oz sugar

12 oz plain flour

1 tsp ginger

1 tsp cinnamon

1½ tsps baking powder

2 eggs (beaten)

A little milk

"Warm the butter, treacle and sugar in a pan until the sugar has dissolved. Mix the flour, ginger, cinnamon and baking powder. Add the liquid from the pan and the beaten eggs. Add the milk. Put into a well greased 7 inch (18 cm) tin. Bake in a moderate oven for 45 minutes." (350°F, Mark 4, 180°C)

GOLDEN MADEIRA CAKE

A simple, classic Madeira cake recipe which keeps well over a few days in an airtight tin.

3 oz sugar

3 oz butter/margarine

2 eggs

A little milk

A few drops vanilla essence

6 oz self raising flour

Pinch of salt

Grated rind of 2 oranges

"Line a 7 inch cake tin. Cream the butter and sugar. Add a little beaten egg and milk. Beat well. Add the rest of the egg, milk, vanilla essence, salt and the flour. Add grated orange rind. If liked, sultanas make a good improvement. Bake in a moderate oven for 1¼ hours."
(350°F, Mark 4, 180°C)

A traditional Ginger Cake

Ginger Cake sliced and ready to enjoy

GROUND RICE CAKE

You will find ground rice in the baking section of any supermarket. The ground rice gives a grainier texture to a cake.

4 eggs

4 oz butter

8 oz sugar

8 oz self raising flour

8 oz ground rice

A few drops lemon essence or rind of one lemon

"Separate the egg whites and whisk well. Beat yolks and butter to a cream with sugar and then mix with the flour and ground rice. Fold in the egg whites. Add the lemon rind or essence. It may be flavoured with essence of almond instead of lemon. Bake for 1 hour."
(325°F, Mark 3, 170°C)

LUNCH CAKE

This cake has an interesting filling not unlike that of the Simnel Cake and reminiscent of Stollen. Finding a slice of this in a picnic basket is a real treat.

½ lb butter

½ lb sugar

4 eggs (beaten)

½ lb self raising flour

½ lb sultanas

Almond paste for the centre:

½ lb ground almonds

½ lb icing sugar

"Beat the butter and sugar to a cream. Add the flour, sultanas and eggs alternately. Leave a little egg for the almond paste. Mix the ground almonds and icing sugar with a little egg to make the paste. Line an 8 inch tin with greaseproof paper. Put in half of the cake mixture, then the rolled out almond paste and then put the remaining cake mixture on top. Bake 1½ hours in a slow oven."
(300°F, Mark 2, 150°C)

MARMALADE SPICE CAKE

Nellie Abson

I love this recipe. I make it regularly now with Grandma Pat's homemade marmalade see VII Chutneys, Pickles, Jams and Jellies page 119, although any marmalade will do, depending on how coarse you like your marmalade.

8 oz self raising flour

3 oz margarine or butter

5 oz marmalade

6 oz golden syrup

2 tsps ginger

1 tsp cinnamon

2 tbsps hot water

1 egg (beaten)

"Grease and line a loaf tin. Melt the margarine (or butter) in the golden syrup in a pan. Mix the flour, ginger and cinnamon. Add the liquid from the pan gradually. Add the marmalade and beaten egg and stir in the hot water. Bake in a warm oven for ¾ hour." (325°F, Mark 3, 170°C)

ORANGE CAKE

Very Good Recipe

Grandma used to make this in a ring tin. I still have one of her ring tins, although it's now slightly dented! I always think of afternoon tea when I remember this one – it's a light textured sponge cake.

5 oz butter

6 oz caster sugar

3 eggs

6 oz self raising flour

Pinch of salt

Grated rind of 1 large orange

Strained juice of ½ orange

"Cream the butter and sugar. Add the eggs (well beaten) and fold in the flour and salt. Lastly, add the orange rind and juice. Beat well and bake for ½ hour in a moderate oven." (375°F, Mark 5, 190°C)

PARKIN RECIPES:

Eating Parkin around Bonfire Night is a Yorkshire custom. Grandma had three recipes, all simple to make. The first gives a superbly tangy ginger flavour; the second is a standard recipe for Parkin. The last one is from Mrs Hick who was the lady of the house where Grandma was in service. She advises that her mixture should be left overnight as Parkin gets better i.e. stickier if you leave it a day or two before eating. We can only wait until it's cool out of the oven!

GINGER PARKIN

12 oz fine oatmeal

4 oz plain flour

1 tsp baking powder

2 tsps ground ginger

3 oz butter

12 oz golden syrup

2 tbsps milk

1 egg

"Sift the flour with the ginger and baking powder and oatmeal. Melt the butter in the golden syrup in a pan. Stir the dry ingredients and add the milk and egg (beaten). Bake in a warm oven for ¾ hour." (300°F, Mark 3, 150°C)

Peppermint Creams
1 lb icing sugar a pinch of carbonate soda
2 ½ tablespoonful cream of tartar mix together
✓ flavour with oil of peppermint roll out
cut into rounds and it is ready for use.

Parkin ✗
1½ lbs medium oatmeal
1 lb flour ½ lb butter, lard or dripping
½ lb sugar 2 teaspoonful Baking Powder
1½ lb treacle 2 teaspoonful ginger
2 egg a little milk Pour treacle on hot

Chorley Cakes
4 ozs plain flour 2 ozs lard pinch of salt
½ teacup of cold water
filling 2ozs currants about ¼ teaspoonful
brown sugar 2 teaspoonful vinegar

Parkin recipe hand written by Grandma Abson

YORKSHIRE PARKIN

8oz self raising flour

1 lb medium oatmeal

1 tsp ginger

Pinch of salt

¼ lb butter

8 oz treacle (could be 4oz black treacle and 4 oz golden syrup)

¼ lb demerara sugar

1 egg beaten

¼ pint milk

"Mix together all of the dry ingredients. Melt the butter in a pan with the treacle and demerara sugar. Mix well with the dry ingredients. Add the egg and milk. Bake in a flat tin in a warm oven for ¾ to 1 hour." (300°F, Mark 3, 150°C)

MRS. HICK'S RECIPE FOR PARKIN

Oakleigh

¼ st oatmeal

½ lb butter

¾ lb demerara sugar

1 tbsp powdered ginger

2 lbs treacle

"Method as Yorkshire Parkin but stand overnight before baking."

Parkin ready to cook in the oven in time for Bonfire Night

Yorkshire Parkin

SIMNEL CAKE

One of my regular seasonal cakes - this one is for Easter Sunday. It's particularly tempting if you decorate it with lots of little chocolate eggs as well as the 11 almond balls. I have some of Grandma's old recipe cuttings where this is often served on Mothering Sunday as well.

4 oz margarine or butter

3 oz sugar

1 tbsp syrup

2 oz ground almonds

2 large eggs (save some of egg white)

1 lb mixed fruit

2 oz chopped peel

2 oz glace cherries

Grated rind of one orange or lemon

8 oz self raising flour

$^1/_4$ tsp salt

$^1/_4$ tsp mixed spice

2-3 tbsp milk

1 lb of almond paste

"Mix all of the ingredients together. Turn half the mixture into a well greased tin and on it place one third of the almond paste, rolled out slightly smaller than the cake measurement. Turn the remaining mixture onto this and bake for 2 - 2$^1/_2$ hours in a slow oven." (300°F, Mark 2, 150°C) "Allow to cool. Then brush the top of the cake with the apricot jam. Roll out half the remaining almond paste and place on top of cake. Shape the remaining almond paste into 11 balls and arrange them around the edge of the cake and brush with egg white. Place under a hot grill or in a very hot oven for 1- 2 minutes to allow top to brown. Then decorate as you like with Easter eggs or decorations."

SAND CAKE

This cake is more like a loaf. It uses cornflour rather than plain or self raising flour and comes out looking smooth and like the colour of golden sand, hence its name.

4 oz sugar

3 oz butter

2 eggs (beaten)

2 oz plain flour

2 oz cornflour

$^1/_2$ tsp baking powder

"Line a loaf tin. Cream the sugar and butter. Add the eggs and beat well. Fold in the flours and baking powder. Bake in a moderate oven for $^1/_2$ - $^3/_4$ hour." (350°F, Mark 4, 180°C)

SPONGE CAKE WITHOUT FAT
Very Old Recipe

This is a recipe which Grandma made in the 1900s. It's a fat free one rather like a modern Swiss Roll recipe. Great for those who are looking to reduce the amount of fat they eat.

2 teacupsful of plain flour

1½ cupful of fine sugar

1 tbsp baking powder

1 cupful of milk

2 eggs

"Beat 2 eggs up and mix with the cup of milk. Then mix all well together. Put into a pudding tin and bake for ¼ of an hour in a quick oven." (375°F, Mark 5, 190°C)

SWISS CAKE

A simple recipe which comes out well each time.

1 cup of sugar

4 oz margarine or butter

2 eggs (beaten)

2 tbsps milk

2 cups of plain flour

1 tsp baking powder

"Beat the sugar, butter, eggs and milk together. Then add the flour and baking powder last. Bake for 20 minutes in a moderate oven." (350°F, Mark 4, 180°C)

VICTORIA SANDWICH

This is Grandma's prize winning recipe from Chapel events. Grandma's take on this classic comes out very light in texture.

3 eggs and their weight in caster sugar, self raising flour and margarine or butter.

Milk to mix.

"Cream the butter and sugar. Beat the eggs and add to the creamed mixture. Fold in the flour. Add the milk. Put into 2 x 7 inch greased tins. Bake for 20 minutes in a quick oven. (375°F, Mark 5, 190°C). When cold, spread raspberry jam on top of one cake and place the other on top. Sprinkle icing sugar on the top cake. Then it will be ready for the table."

II – Buns

For those of you new to baking, making buns is a fun way to get into baking whatever your age. Given a basin and a wooden spoon, many children start off baking buns as a first step to cooking and will remember making 'Butterfly Buns' at school. Grandma had a good repertoire of small cakes (or 'buns' as they are called in Yorkshire) which were made following similar methods as described in the 'cakes' section. Sometimes her recipes have a practical side: Lunch Buns and Useful Buns! It is essential to equip yourself with a couple of bun tins or trays, baking paper or parchment and paper bun cases for the mixture. Nowadays, silicone bun cases are an excellent alternative. Some recipes also refer to rice paper. This is an edible baking paper which is often used for sticky baked cakes or buns.

Grandma's elder sister, Emma Tooth, regularly made Coconut Buns or plain Rock Buns when my sister and I stayed during summer holidays at her home in Manchester. Grandma's youngest sister, Ivy Henderson, excelled in Coconut Macaroons and brought them when she came to visit us in Bolton-on-Dearne.

I like to make Raspberry Buns (which you can still buy in cake shops in Barnsley). Ground rice, which features in this recipe and a number of other recipes for cakes and buns, is often mixed with flour or ground almonds. It enriches the baking to give a slightly different and grainier texture. You can get traditional ingredients like this in the baking section in most big supermarkets.

Christmas Mince Pies

Contents

Ginger Buns

ALMOND CAKES

These fingers with the almond flakes on top are a real teatime treat.

4 oz butter

4 oz sugar

3 oz plain flour

1 tsp baking powder

2 oz ground almonds

2 eggs

2 oz roughly chopped and browned almonds

Icing sugar

"Beat the butter and sugar to a cream, add each egg separately and beat well. Sift the flour, baking powder and ground almonds together and stir lightly into the creamed mixture. Spread in a shallow baking tin lined with greased paper. Bake for 35 minutes in a warm oven." (300°F, Mark 3, 150°C) "When cold, sieve the icing sugar over and sprinkle with browned almonds. Cut into finger lengths."

BUTTERFLY BUNS

An old favourite and one of the first recipes to make when you start baking with young children.

2 oz margarine or butter

2 oz sugar

1 egg

2 tsp lemon essence

3 oz self raising flour

1 level tsp baking powder

A little milk

"Cream the margarine or butter and sugar and add the essence and beaten egg. Sift the flour and baking powder and add to the creamed mixture using a little milk if necessary. Half fill greased patty tins and bake in a moderate oven for 15 minutes." (350°F, Mark 4, 180°C) "Scoop out the top of each bun and fill the hole with butter cream (see VI Sauces, Icings and Fillings page 111). Replace the scooped out sponge as a lid. Dust with icing sugar."

CHORLEY CAKES

These small cakes are an alternative to Eccles cakes and less complicated; make sure the pastry is light by chilling before rolling out and then keeping it cool before cooking.

Pastry

4 oz plain flour

2 oz lard or butter

Pinch of salt

Half teacup of cold water

Filling

2 oz currants

4 tsp brown sugar

2 tsp vinegar

"Make the pastry (See V Puddings page 101). Roll out the pastry and cut out into rounds. Place the rounds in a bun tin. Mix together the currants, brown sugar and vinegar for the filling. Place a teaspoonful of the filling in each case. Cover with a pastry lid. Bake in a fairly hot oven for 20 minutes." (400°F, Mark 6, 200°C)

COCONUT MACAROONS
Ivy Henderson

If you like coconut, these are a delight. Make sure the egg whites are really stiff to ensure a sticky texture once cooked.

Whites of 2 eggs

4 oz desiccated coconut

2 oz sugar

1 tbsp self raising flour

"Whisk the egg whites until stiff. Mix the other ingredients together. Fold in the dry ingredients into the egg whites. Place teaspoonfuls of the mixture on rice paper. Bake on a tray for 20 minutes."
(350°F, Mark 4, 180°C)

COCONUT ROCK BUNS

Emma Tooth

I always think of teatime at Chorlton cum Hardy in Manchester at Auntie Emma's. This was one of her signature recipes. See also Rock Buns later on page 58 in II Buns.

4 oz butter or margarine

12 oz self raising flour

Pinch of salt

4 oz desiccated coconut

4 oz sugar

1 egg

¼ pint of milk

"Rub the butter or margarine into the flour and salt. Add the sugar and coconut. Add the egg (beaten) and milk and mix well. Put on a greased tin or on greased baking sheets and shape into small rocky heaps with two forks. Bake in a moderate oven for 20 minutes." (350°F, Mark 4, 180°C)

COFFEE BUNS

Large Quantity

These are a tease – not made with coffee but with currants! These 'buns' are to have with your elevenses. The quantities mean you can make a large batch but you'll find they soon disappear!

1½ lb sugar

1½ lb margarine

4 eggs

3 lb plain flour

½ oz baking powder

9 oz currants

"Mix the sugar and margarine to a cream. Beat the eggs and add gradually to the mixture. Mix the baking powder, flour and currants and fold into the mixture. Bake in a moderate oven for 20 minutes." (350°F, Mark 4, 180°C)

CURRANT BUNS

A regular favourite – as children, we always liked to count how many currants we had in the bun we were eating!

½ lb self raising flour

¼ lb margarine or butter

¼ lb sugar

¼ lb currants

2 eggs

2 tsps milk

"Rub the fat into the flour. Add the sugar and currants. Beat the eggs and add to the mixture. Add the milk. Bake for 15 minutes in a quick oven." (375°F, Mark 5, 190°C)

FAIRY CAKES

A quick and easy favourite which has a light texture.

3 oz butter

3 oz sugar

1 egg

5 oz plain flour

1 tsp baking powder

"Mix the butter and sugar to a cream. Beat the egg. Add the egg to the creamed butter and sugar, together with flour, the baking powder being mixed into the last spoonful. Form into balls and sprinkle with caster sugar. Bake in a quick oven for 10 minutes." (300°F, Mark 3, 150°C)

GINGER BUNS

A lighter alternative recipe to the Parkin recipes. See I Cakes page 44. You could make these as larger buns in muffin cases nowadays but allow another 8 to 10 minutes cooking time.

2 oz margarine or butter

2 dsps treacle

2 oz sugar

4 oz plain flour

1 tsp ginger

1 tsp baking powder

1 egg

A little milk to mix

"Spread 12 bun cases in a baking tray. Melt the margarine or butter in a pan over a low heat and add the treacle and sugar until blended. Mix together the dry ingredients - flour, ginger, baking powder. Mix together the egg and the milk and add to the other liquid when slightly cooled. Make a well in the centre of the dry ingredients and add the liquid. Mix well. Fill the bun cases with the mixture. Bake in a moderate oven for 20 minutes." (350°F, Mark 4, 180°C)

GROUND RICE BUNS

Very Nice Recipe

The ground rice gives a grainy texture to the normal sponge mixture – these buns have a hint of lemon.

1 cupful of plain flour

1 cupful of sugar

1 cupful of ground rice

1 egg

A little milk

1/2 cup of butter

1 tsp baking powder

Lemon essence

"Mix together the dry ingredients. Break the butter into small pieces and rub into the dry ingredients until they are like breadcrumbs. Add the egg (beaten), milk and lemon essence. Bake in a moderate oven in greased bun tins for 20 minutes." (350°F, Mark 4, 180°C)

GROUND RICE CHEESECAKES

They are a bit like mini Bakewell tarts. Grandma always used homemade jam for these such as Raspberry Jam. See VII Chutney, Pickles and Jams on page 121.

2 oz butter

2 oz sugar

1 egg

2 oz ground rice

A few drops of lemon essence

(Raspberry) Jam as required

Shortcrust pastry

"Cream the sugar and butter. Add the beaten egg and ground rice. Lastly, add the lemon essence. Line the tartlet or bun tins with pastry. Place a layer of jam between the pastry and the mixture. Put a good teaspoonful of the mixture in each. Bake in a fairly hot oven until golden brown." (400°F, Mark 6, 200°C)

LONDON BUNS

Ivy Henderson

Grandma's sister, Ivy, picked up this recipe up on a trip to London but we never found out where she went for afternoon tea.

1 lb plain flour

6 oz butter or lard

$\frac{1}{2}$ tsp salt

2 tsps baking powder

8 oz sugar

Grated rind of 1 lemon

2 eggs

$\frac{1}{4}$ pint of milk

"Rub the fat into the flour, salt and baking powder. Add the sugar and grated lemon rind. Beat the eggs and add to the mixture. Add enough milk to give a soft consistency. Bake in a fairly hot oven for 15 minutes." (400°F, Mark 6, 200°C)

LUNCH BUNS

These are something to look forward to alongside a sandwich and piece of fruit in your sandwich box.

9 oz sugar

6 oz margarine or butter

2 eggs

14 oz plain flour

2 tsps baking powder

3 oz currants

$\frac{1}{4}$ pint of milk

"Cream the sugar and margarine or butter. Beat the eggs and add gradually. Add the flour and baking powder. Add the currants and milk and mix. Bake in a fairly hot oven for 20 minutes." (400°F, Mark 6, 200°C)

MACAROONS
Very Good Recipe

This recipe gives a pleasant alternative, if you don't like coconut.

4 oz caster sugar

2 oz ground almonds

1 tsp ground rice

A few drops of almond essence

Split almonds

White of a large egg

"Mix the sugar, ground almonds and ground rice together. Add the essence and unbeaten white of egg. Mix to a stiff paste. Beat well and place a teaspoonful of the mixture on rice paper spread on a baking tray. Place a few split almonds on top. Bake for 25 minutes in a slow oven."
(300°F, Mark 2, 150°C)

MINCE PIES:

These are always a Christmas favourite and so delicious. You can always adjust the amount of sugar in the mincemeat if, like me, you don't have a sweet tooth. I make 2 trays of mince pies in the last couple of days before Christmas, using the quantities in Grandma's Shortcrust pastry with egg in V Puddings, Pastry and Desserts page 101. We warm them up quickly to have with mulled wine for a real taste of Christmas.

Shortcrust pastry
See V Puddings, Pastry and Desserts page 101

Mincemeat
See VII Chutneys, Pickles and Jams page 120

"Line pastry tins with shortcrust pastry rounds. Put 2 teaspoonfuls of mincemeat into each one. Moisten the edge with milk. Cover with lids. Prick each lid with a fork. Bake in a moderate oven for 10-15 minutes."
(350°F, Mark 4, 180°C)

MOCK CURD TARTS

These are a mini version of the famous Yorkshire Curd Tart.

Short crust pastry
(see V Puddings, Pastry and Desserts page 101)

Filling
3 oz butter

3 oz currants

3 oz sugar

1 hard boiled egg (chopped finely)

1 dsp ground rice

A little vanilla essence

1 egg

"For the filling, mix the ingredients well together. Line small patty tins with short crust pastry and fill with the mixture. It will brown when baked, looking exactly like curd. A little nutmeg may be added if desired. Bake in a moderate oven for 20 minutes." (350°F, Mark 4, 180°C)

QUEEN CAKES

Another variant on the various currant buns – fit for Royalty.

4 oz butter

4 oz sugar

2 eggs

6 oz self raising flour

Pinch of salt

4 oz currants

2 tbsps milk

"Arrange 16-20 paper cases on a baking tray. Beat the butter until soft. Add the sugar and cream together until the mixture is pale and fluffy. Add the eggs (well beaten) gradually. Fold in the flour and salt. Then, stir in the fruit. Add the milk. Put the mixture into baking cases and half fill them. Bake for 15-20 minutes in fairly hot oven." (375°F, Mark 5, 190°C)

"You can brush over the top with egg and place a small piece of lump sugar over each one."

RASPBERRY BUNS

A good recipe to try with children. They love to make a hole in the centre with their (clean) finger and spoon in the Raspberry Jam.

6 oz plain flour

4 oz butter or lard

6 oz ground rice

4 oz sugar

1 tsp baking powder

2 eggs (leaving out 1 white)

Pinch of salt

Milk to mix

Raspberry jam

"Rub the butter into the flour and then add the ground rice, sugar, baking powder, salt and eggs (well beaten) and milk. Mix to a stiff consistency. Form small buns from the dough and put these on well greased tins. Brush over with the white of egg. Put a little jam in the centre of each. Bake for 20 minutes in a fairly hot oven." (400°F, Mark 6, 200°C)

ROCK BUNS
Emma Tooth

This time without the coconut. See also Coconut Rock Buns earlier on page 52 in II Buns. This was Auntie Emma's regular teatime recipe.

¾ lb plain flour

2 tsps baking powder

¼ lb butter or lard

Pinch of salt

¼ lb sugar

¼ lb currants or raisins

2 eggs

1 teacupful of milk

"Sieve the baking powder with the flour. Rub the fat into flour and salt then add the sugar and the fruit. Beat the eggs and add these to the mixture with the milk. Mix well. Put on a greased tin or on greased baking sheets and shape into small rocky heaps with two forks. Bake for 20 minutes in a fairly hot oven." (400°F, Mark 6, 200°C)

SULTANA BUNS

Clara Cave

These buns have a lighter texture than scones but the sultanas keep the buns moist over several days in the same way.

2 oz butter

8 oz plain flour

1 tbsp baking powder

4 oz sugar

4 oz sultanas

2 oz candied/mixed peel

2 eggs

A little milk

"Rub the butter into the flour and baking powder. Add the sugar, sultanas and mixed peel. Beat the eggs. Mix in, together with a little milk. Put a dessertspoonful in each bun case. Bake in moderate oven for 15-20 minutes."
(350°F, Mark 4, 180°C)

USEFUL BUNS

Grandma's baking always had a leaning towards the 'practical'. These buns clearly served a 'useful' purpose.

1 lb plain flour

4 oz butter or lard

4 oz sugar

4 oz currants or sultanas

2 large tsps baking powder

2 eggs

A little milk

"Sieve the baking powder with the flour. Rub the fat into the flour and salt, then add the sugar and the fruit. Beat the eggs and add these to the mixture with a little milk. Bake for 15-20 minutes in a moderate oven."
(350°F, Mark 4, 180°C)

VANILLA CAKES

The lemon peel and vanilla give a citrus taste. Grandma never went abroad but these cakes remind me of the smell of small lemon sponge cakes I've eaten in Provence.

2 eggs

Their weight in sugar

Half their weight in self raising flour

Mixed spice to taste

Vanilla essence

Grated lemon peel

"Beat the yolks of the eggs and the sugar together. Whisk the whites to a froth and add these and the flour slowly. Add the mixed spice, vanilla essence and grated lemon peel. Put a teaspoonful of the mixture in a bun case for each one. Bake for 3 to 5 minutes in a moderate oven."
(350°F, Mark 4, 180°C).

III – Teabreads and Scones

This section includes a wide range of those things which make afternoon tea a delight. Most of these recipes are made in loaf tins which are now available in non stick versions. Once sliced and spread with butter, teabreads and scones melt in the mouth. My favourites include Banana Nut Bread, Eccles Cakes and Scones. The recipe for Fruit Harvo from the initial collection of Grandma's recipes has featured on Nigella Lawson's website and described as 'A nice sticky malty loaf, which keeps well' as it appears 'in the book that I have (Grandma Abson's Yorkshire recipes)'. Grandma would have been very pleased to see her recipe shared and adapted in this way.

Some of the other recipes use yeast as a key ingredient such as Hot Cross Buns, Sally Lunns and Teacakes. Grandma would usually use fresh yeast but nowadays we can easily get easy blend or active yeasts which are just as convenient. Remember dried yeast is more concentrated so use half the quantity given in these recipes.

Contents

BANANA NUT BREAD
Nellie Abson

Nellie (Grandma's daughter-in-law) shared a number of recipes with Grandma during the 1950s and 60s. Once bananas were available after rationing ended after the Second World War, this recipe was a firm favourite. The bananas keep it moist whilst the walnuts give it a crunchy texture.

8 oz self raising flour
Pinch of salt
2 oz margarine or butter
2 oz caster sugar
2 oz chopped walnuts
1 egg (beaten)
3 oz golden syrup (warmed)
2 bananas (mashed)

"Sift the flour and salt. Rub in the margarine/butter. Add the sugar and walnuts. Blend the egg with the warmed golden syrup and stir in the mashed bananas. Add to the dry ingredients and mix well. Turn into a greased loaf tin. Bake for 1 hour."
(350°F, Mark 4, 180°C)

BUTTERED CAKE

This is a simple fruit teabread recipe. Just spread with butter once it's cool from out of the oven and it's ready to serve.

8 oz self raising flour
1 handful of dried mixed fruit
2 tbsps golden syrup (warmed)
1 tbsp marmalade
Pinch of salt
Milk to mix

"Mix all together – not too stiff. Bake in a warm oven for 1 hour."
(325°F, Mark 3, 165°C)

ECCLES CAKES

Eccles Cakes are quite complicated to make but here, Grandma does leave quite clear instructions. I like to put in plenty of currants so the pastry isn't too overwhelming.

8 oz plain flour

Pinch of salt

5 oz fat (mixture of butter and lard)

Squeeze of lemon juice

8 tbsps water

"Mix the flour and salt. Work one quarter of the fat into the flour until it becomes breadcrumbs. Add enough water to make the dough. Roll out the dough – then put the second quarter of fat (cut into pieces) onto the pastry and fold over, adding water as required. Roll out and leave to rest in a cool place. Repeat with rest of the fat until all is used. Add a squeeze of lemon juice. Leave to rest for another 30 minutes. Roll out the dough and cut into rounds (8-10) about 3 inches diameter.

Filling:

4 oz currants

1 dsp caster sugar

1 oz butter

Put 1 tsp of filling in each round. Leave for ½ hour. Bake for 20 minutes in a hot oven".
(425°F, Mark 7, 210°C)

FRUIT HARVO

While doing some research for this new edition, I was delighted to find that this recipe from the original edition of 'Grandma Abson's Yorkshire Recipes' had been posted on Nigella Lawson's website. It was described as 'A nice sticky malty loaf, which keeps well'. It's actually a teabread, made with lots of sultanas, which you can spread with butter, although it's really delicious on its own. The writer comments on measuring using cups rather than scales. Don't be afraid of using a cup as a measurement. This old-fashioned technique really works.

½ lb margarine

1 lb sultanas

1½ cups of sugar

4 cups of plain flour

3 tsps bicarbonate of soda

3 tsps baking powder

1 tsp ginger

2 cups water

"Put the margarine, sultanas and sugar into a saucepan and cover with 2 cups of water. Bring to the boil. Then simmer for 10 minutes. Allow to cool. Mix together the flour, baking powder, bicarbonate of soda and ginger. Stir the liquid from the pan into the dry ingredients. Put into well greased loaf tins. Bake for 1½ hours in a warm oven."
(325°F, Mark 3, 165°C)

HARVO BREAD

This is one of those recipes with a 'cup of this and that'. People tell me they love them because they are so simple and that there is no need to weigh out all the ingredients.

2 cups brown flour

2 cups white plain flour

1 cup syrup or treacle

1 cup sugar

1 cup raisins

1 tsp bicarbonate of soda

Milk to mix

"Mix the ingredients together with milk to a soft paste. Pour into greased loaf tins. Bake in a slow oven for 2 hours." (300°F, Mark 2, 150°C)

HOT CROSS BUNS

On Good Friday, Grandma would leave the dough to rise on the hearth near the range. We can use the airing cupboard, a sunny windowsill or a warm place near a radiator.

1 oz yeast

$^1/_2$ pint scalded milk

1 lb plain flour

1 tsp salt

1 tsp mixed spice

$1^1/_2$ oz sugar

2 oz margarine or butter

1 egg

2 oz currants

"Blend the yeast with the milk. Mix the flour, salt and mixed spice. Stir in the sugar. Make a well in the centre and add the margarine/butter, egg and yeast mixture. Add the currants and mix to a soft dough. Knead for 10 minutes or so until smooth. Cover with a tea towel. Leave to rise in a warm place until doubled in size. Turn out and knead for 2-3 minutes. Cut the dough into 10-12 pieces and shape into buns. Place on a greased baking tray and put in a warm place until doubled in size. Make a small amount of shortcrust pastry (see V Puddings, Pastry and Desserts page 101), roll out and cut into thin strips. Brush with milk and place across each bun to make a cross. Bake in a hot oven (425°F, Mark 7, 210°C) for 15 minutes. Brush with a glaze made from milk and sugar and allow to cool."

HUBBARD TEA CAKES
Mrs Hubbard

Grandma has written that this is a recipe of Mrs Hubbard's from Doncaster but sadly the rest is an unsolved mystery. These tea cakes come out rather like small flat sponge cakes similar to a brioche. They are delicious.

12 oz plain flour

2 tsp baking powder

4 oz sugar

4 oz lard

2 eggs

A little milk

A few drops of almond essence

"Mix the dry ingredients together. Rub in the fat. Moisten with the eggs and milk. Add the almond essence. Bake in shallow round tins in a warm oven for about 20 minutes. Serve hot and well buttered."
(325°F, Mark 3, 170°C)

SALLY LUNNS

This was Grandma's version of the original Sally Lunn bun from Bath.

1 lb plain flour

1 oz yeast

2 oz sugar

4 oz butter

2 eggs

Pinch of salt

1 tsp bicarbonate of soda

A few currants (if desired)

½ pint of milk

"Cream the yeast with 1 tsp sugar and 1 tsp flour. Add half the milk and let it stand for 10 minutes in a warm place to rise. Melt the butter in the rest of the milk. Beat the eggs and mix with it. Then stir in the yeast mixture. Sift the flour, bicarbonate of soda, sugar and salt and currants together. Make a hole in the centre. Pour in the yeast mixture and stir with a spoon. Grease 3 tins and divide the mixture between each one. Stand on a baking shelf in a warm place for about an hour until level with the top of the tin. Bake in a hot oven for 15 to 20 minutes."
(425°F, Mark 7, 220°C)

SCONES

Grandma's scones always came out light and airy and won many plaudits. I like to taste different varieties of scones but always return to this recipe. The sultanas keep them moist.

8 oz self raising flour

¹/₂ tsp salt

2 oz margarine or butter

2 oz sugar

2 oz sultanas

2 eggs

Milk to mix

"Add the salt to the flour. Rub in the margarine/butter. Add the sugar and sultanas. Beat the eggs and milk and add to make a dough. Roll out and cut into sections with a cutter.
Bake for 10-12 minutes on the third runner from the top of the oven."
(450°F, Mark 8, 230°C)

SCONES
Large Quantity

Grandma had to make large quantities when she was in service and you can see that it wasn't just a matter of doubling up quantities. There were savings to be made in some ingredients when making a large batch.

2 lbs self raising flour

6 oz margarine or butter

4 eggs

9 oz sultanas

6 oz sugar

Milk to mix

"Method as before."

SCOTCH PANCAKES

This recipe makes a tasty treat and an interesting alternative to scones. Serve them with golden syrup or jam.

6 oz plain flour

1 dsp caster sugar

1 egg

Milk to mix

½ tsp cream of tartar

¼ tsp bicarbonate of soda

"Mix the flour and sugar. Make a well in the centre. Break in the egg and beat in the milk gradually. Make a thick batter. Lastly add the cream of tartar and bicarbonate of soda. Slightly grease the top of a griddle plate and drop the mixture in dessertspoonfuls on to the griddle. Cook on one side, then turn and cook the other. You can use a thick frying pan instead."

SULTANA LOAF

This is an easy to mix recipe and makes a moist loaf.

½ lb margarine or butter

1 lb sultanas

1½ cups of sugar

2 cups water

4 cups plain flour

6 tsps baking powder

1½ tsps bicarbonate of soda

1 tsp ginger

"Put the margarine/butter, sultanas and sugar in a saucepan and cover with 2 cups of water. Bring to the boil. Then simmer for 10 minutes. Allow to cool. Mix together the flour, baking powder, bicarbonate of soda and ginger. Stir the liquid from the pan into the dry ingredients. Put into well greased loaf tins. Bake for 1½ hours in a warm oven."

(325°F, Mark 3, 170°C)

TEACAKES

There is nothing better on a cold rainy day than freshly toasted hot teacakes with melting butter. I always prefer to add the currants for that extra bit of extravagance.

1 oz yeast

$\frac{1}{2}$ pint of milk

A little sugar

1 lb plain flour

2 oz lard

Pinch of salt

4 oz currants if desired

"Blend the yeast with the milk and sugar. Mix together the flour and salt and rub in the fat. Stir in the yeast liquid and mix until a firm dough. Add the currants if desired.
Knead for 5 minutes or so. Place in a bowl and cover with a tea towel. Leave until double in size. Lightly knead for 2-3 minutes and cut into 10 pieces. Shape into a ball and place on a greased baking tray. Cover with a tea towel and leave in a warm place until doubled in size again. Bake in a hot oven until golden."
(425°F, Mark 7, 220°C)

WISCARD GINGERBREAD

This is a simple recipe which I love since it has that ginger piquant taste. We have no detail about the origins of 'Wiscard'.

$\frac{1}{2}$ lb plain flour

1 level tsp bicarbonate of soda

1 tsp ginger

3 oz butter

3 tbsps treacle (warmed)

3 tbsp golden syrup

3 oz demerara sugar

1 cup of warm water

1 egg beaten

"Mix together all of the dry ingredients in a bowl. Melt the butter in a pan with the treacle, golden syrup and the sugar until the sugar has dissolved. Do not allow to boil.
Make a well in the dry ingredients and pour in the mixture from the pan. Add the water and the beaten egg and mix well. Turn into a well greased flat tin. Bake in a warm oven for about 1 hour." (325°F, Mark 3, 170°C)

IV – Biscuits, Sweets and Toffee

Biscuits are really quick and easy to make and they are a treat to have in your biscuit tin. They generally don't demand a lot of time and effort. As well as some classic biscuits such as Brandy Snaps for grown ups and crowd pleasers like Shortbreads and Ginger Snaps, Grandma made a lot of biscuits using dried fruit and dates which go perfectly with a cup of tea or coffee. Grandma's sister Clara Cave, who tragically died in the 1930s, left a tiny red notebook with her recipes written down neatly. She had a real talent for making biscuits which were consumed almost as soon as they came out of the oven. The trick with modern ovens is not to leave them in for too long so they don't get too hard when they are cool. Grandma always used baking parchment or greaseproof paper to line the baking trays to make it easier to remove the biscuits. Then she put them onto wire trays. I like Clara's recipes for Butter Biscuits and German Biscuits. Other favourites of mine are the Coconut Fingers, Date Crispy or Date Squares and Oat Ginger Biscuits.

Making sweets and toffee at home is much less common now than in Grandma's day as factory produced confectionery is so common everywhere. The recipes in this section are simple and cheap to produce. Grandma used to make sweets and toffees with us when we were children, especially Treacle Toffee around Bonfire Night. These are good to eat but watch your teeth! If you try these recipes with children, make sure you keep the pans well away from the edge of the hob and be careful not to let them touch the melted sugary mixture as melted toffee can cause severe burns. My favourites are Peppermint Creams and the more exotic Pineapple Fudge from Nellie Abson (Grandma's daughter-in-law) which also went down well with a glass of Lemon Barley in summer.

Contents

BISCUITS:

BRANDY SNAPS

This is a real old favourite. Grandma used to grease the handles of several wooden spoons ready to roll the mixture around. You can serve these with ice cream and fruit or with any of the cold desserts in V Puddings, Pastries and Desserts. For a thoroughly 'naughty but nice' delectable treat, fill them with whipped double cream.

2 oz butter
2 oz demerara sugar
2 oz golden syrup
½ tsp ginger
2 oz flour
½ tsp lemon juice

"Warm the butter, sugar, syrup and ginger gently in a saucepan until the butter is melted. Sift in the flour and add the lemon juice. Grease a baking tin and pour teaspoonfuls of the mixture at a good distance apart to form rounds. Bake for 15 minutes in a moderate oven." (350°F, Mark 4, 180°C) "Lift off the tin with a knife and roll round a wooden spoon handle quickly."

BUTTER BISCUITS
Clara Cave

A simple biscuit similar to shortbread but thinner.

¼ lb plain flour
¼ lb butter
2 oz caster sugar
Yolk of 1 small egg

"Rub the butter well into the flour and sugar. Then mix it well with the yolk of the egg to make a paste. Cut the paste with a small pastry cutter and bake the biscuits in a quick oven for 15 minutes." (375°F, Mark 5, 190°C)

CHOCOLATE BISCUITS
Clara Cave

Who can resist these homemade chocolate biscuits which melt in the mouth?

¼ lb chocolate
1 oz plain flour
2 oz sugar
4 oz butter
1 egg

"Mix all well together into a paste and cut the paste with a cutter. Bake in a moderately quick oven for 15-20 minutes." (375°F, Mark 5, 190°C)

CHOCOLATE COOKIES

Grandma refers to 'patty tins' which are simply baking tins, usually used for jam tarts or mince pies. It's important to grease them well or use bun cases or silicone moulds for these cookies.

2 oz margarine or butter

2 oz sugar

1 egg

4 oz plain flour

A pinch of salt

1 level tsp baking powder

1 level tbsp cocoa

A little milk and water

A few drops of vanilla essence

"Cream the fat, sugar and egg. Add the flour mixed with the baking powder, cocoa and salt, and mix to a soft consistency with milk and water. Add the vanilla essence. Put into greased patty tins and bake in a quick oven for 15 to 20 minutes." (375°F, Mark 5, 190°C)

COCONUT FINGERS

If you like coconut, these are irresistible. Cut them into fingers while they are still warm, and then leave to cool in the tin.

4 oz butter

4 oz sugar

2 eggs (beaten)

4 oz plain flour

¼ oz baking powder

6 oz coconut

"Cream the butter and sugar. Add the eggs, flour and baking powder. Then add the coconut. Mix well and bake in a flat tin in a quick oven for 20-25 minutes." (375°F, Mark 5, 190°C)

CURLED GINGERBREAD

These gingerbreads are an alternative to Brandy Snaps. Grandma used to grease the handles of several wooden spoons ready to roll the mixture around.

½ lb plain flour

¼ lb butter

½ lb brown sugar

1 tbsp ground ginger

1 lb treacle

Juice of one lemon

"Rub the butter into the flour.
Add the sugar and ginger. Mix well.
Then add the treacle and lemon juice.
Put teaspoonfuls of the mixture on
well greased tins. Bake in a moderate
oven for 15 minutes."
(375°F, Mark 5, 190°C)
"When cooked, roll around a wooden
spoon handle, and slip off when set."

DATE CRISPY or DATE SQUARES

If you don't like dates in this recipe, it works just as well with dried apricots. Scrumptious!

3 oz margarine

1 oz sugar

6 oz cooking dates (cut up)

8 oz cooking chocolate

2 oz rice crispies

"Melt the margarine, sugar and
dates in a pan until soft. Divide the
chocolate into two. Melt half of it
and add to the date mixture. Stir in
the rice crispies. Line a baking tin and
press into the tin. Melt the rest of the
chocolate and put on top. Leave to
cool and cut into fingers."

GERMAN BISCUITS
Clara Cave

This is a very simple recipe from Clara's tiny red notebook. Keep them crisp by storing them in an airtight tin.

½ lb butter

½ lb caster sugar

½ lb plain flour

2 or 3 eggs (according to size)

A little vanilla or rind of a lemon

"Mix all together and make into
small biscuits. Bake in a quick oven
for 15-20 minutes."
(375°F, Mark 5, 190°C)

GINGER SNAPS

These biscuits are best left to cool for a few minutes before removing from the baking tray as they should be still a little soft when just out of the oven. Then put them onto a wire rack.

4 oz plain flour

1 tsp bicarbonate of soda

4 oz oatmeal

½ tsp cinnamon

1 tsp ginger

2 oz lard or margarine

1 egg

2 oz golden syrup

"Mix the flour, bicarbonate of soda, oatmeal, cinnamon and ginger. Rub the fat into the flour until like breadcrumbs. Beat the egg and add the golden syrup. Stir into the mixture to form a paste. Roll out and cut into rounds. Bake in a quick oven for 15 – 20 minutes."
(375°F, Mark 5, 190°C)

GRANTHAM BISCUITS

These biscuits have a similar taste to Ginger Snaps but they are cooked at a lower temperature. Break off small pieces into the palm of your hands and mould into small rounds as Grandma describes. Wet your hands with a little water if the dough sticks to them. An old penny was quite large – slightly bigger than a 50p piece.

½ lb margarine or butter

1 lb sugar

1 lb plain flour

1 tbsp ginger

1 tsp bicarbonate of soda

1 egg (beaten)

"Cream the margarine/butter and sugar. Add the ginger and the bicarbonate of soda to the flour. Add the egg to the creamed mixture and then fold in the flour. Make into a stiff dough. Roll out and make into rounds – the size of a penny. Bake in a slow oven for 30 minutes."
(300°F, Mark 2, 150°C)

JUMBLES

The name 'Jumbles' refers to the irregular shapes. You can also make any shape you like including letters of the alphabet such as 'S' shapes. These are fun to make with children as they can create their own shapes.

1 lb butter

1 lb sugar

Vanilla essence or grated lemon rind

4 eggs (beaten)

1½ lb self raising flour

"Cream the butter and sugar. Add the vanilla essence or grated lemon rind, then the eggs and flour. Mix to a stiff paste. Make into fancy shapes. Roughen the top of each shape with a fork and bake on a well greased tray. Bake for 20 minutes in a quick oven." (375°F, Mark 5, 190°C)

OATMEAL BISCUITS

These always turn out deliciously crisp and fresh but keep well over several days if you put them in an airtight tin.

¼ lb oatmeal

½ lb self raising flour

2 tsps baking powder

½ tsp ginger

¼ lb butter or lard

¼ lb sugar

1 good sized cup of milk

"Mix together the oatmeal, flour, baking powder and ginger with the fat, add the sugar and the milk to mix. Roll out into biscuits and place on a baking tray. Bake in a quick oven for 20 minutes." (375°F, Mark 5, 190°C)

OAT GINGER BISCUITS

These are similar to Oatmeal biscuits but this time, Grandma uses porridge or rolled oats rather than the finer oatmeal, so they have a chewier texture.

¼ cup margarine or butter

1 tbsp golden syrup

¾ cup of sugar

¾ cup of plain flour

1 tsp bicarbonate of soda

¾ cup oats

½ tsp ginger

2 tbsps water

"Melt the margarine/butter with the golden syrup and sugar in a pan over a low heat. Mix the dry ingredients (flour, bicarbonate of soda and ginger) and add to the melted mixture.
Mix well and add the water.
Roll into rounds on a well greased baking tray. Bake in a quick oven for 15 - 20 minutes. Remove from the baking tray while warm."
(375°F, Mark 5, 190°C)

SCOTCH SHORTBREAD

This is a traditional recipe for shortbread using ground rice. It gives a grainier texture to the mixture. Bake these until golden brown for a melt in the mouth moment. Once cooked, mark out fingers of shortbread in the tray with a knife so they will break off easily when cool. Then prick each one several times with a fork to make a pattern on the top.

½ lb butter

¼ lb sugar

1 lb plain flour

2 oz ground rice

"Melt the butter. Add the sugar and gradually add the flour and ground rice together. Roll out onto a tray lined with greased paper. Bake in a slow oven for around 30 minutes."
(300°F, Mark 2, 150°C)

SHORTBREAD BISCUITS

This recipe is for individual shortbread biscuits which should be even in size and shape. The cherry makes a tantalising topping. Will you eat the cherry first like I used to?

10 oz butter

1 lb plain flour

6 oz caster sugar

1 pinch of salt

1 or 2 yolks of eggs

Glace cherries

"Rub the butter into the flour and add the sugar and the salt. Then add the egg and work into the flour as quickly as possible, making a dry dough. The mixture must be kept dry. Roll out an inch thick and cut into rounds. Put a cherry in the centre. Bake for 25 minutes in a slow oven." (300˚F, Mark 2, 150˚C)

SHREWSBURY BISCUITS

Grandma's recipe is for plain Shrewsbury Biscuits but I remember she did say you could add 2oz (50g) currants for Fruit Shrewsbury Biscuits.

4 oz margarine or butter

3 oz sugar

6 oz plain flour

1 tsp cinnamon or rind of a lemon

1 egg (beaten)

"Cream the fat and sugar. Mix the cinnamon into the flour. Then add the flour and egg alternately. Roll out ¼ inch thick and cut into rounds. Bake in a quick oven to a golden colour for 15 minutes." (375˚F, Mark 5, 190˚C)

SWEET BISCUITS

A simple recipe. You can also reduce the amount of sugar if, like me, you don't have a sweet tooth. Keep the 'paste' cool before cooking so the biscuits don't reduce in size.

1 lb plain flour

1 large tsp baking powder

4 oz butter

4 oz sugar

2 eggs (beaten)

2 tbsps milk

"Mix the flour with the baking powder and rub in the butter. Add the sugar and the eggs and milk to form a paste. Roll out thinly. Cut into rounds. Bake in a quick oven for 15 minutes." (375°F, Mark 5, 190°C)

WHITE GINGERBREAD

Grandma mentions a 'sheet iron' in the instructions for this recipe – this is simply a thin metal baking tray. These biscuits are not white but lighter in colour than the usual gingerbread. The pieces should be around the size of a walnut. Keep them well spaced apart on the tray otherwise they may merge together when cooking.

1 lb plain flour

½ lb ground rice

1 lb white sugar

1 tsp ground ginger

2 oz butter

1 tsp baking powder

12 drops lemon essence

2 eggs

A little milk to mix

"Work all the ingredients together into a paste which must be stiff enough to roll out and cut into rounds or finger pieces. Drop these onto a sheet iron with a teaspoon. Bake in a quick oven for 15 minutes." (375°F, Mark 5, 190°C)

SWEETS:

MELTING MOMENTS

'Patty' tin is another name for a bun or small cake tin with individual indentations. It's a good idea to use small bun cases or sweet papers (preferably waxed) in the tins.

6 oz butter

3 oz caster sugar

2 eggs

8 oz cornflour

1 small tsp baking powder

"Beat the butter and sugar to a cream. Add the eggs (well beaten). Mix in the other ingredients and beat all well together. Drop into small patty tins in teaspoonfuls. Makes 30. Bake for 20 minutes in a quick oven."
(375°F, Mark 5, 190°C)

MINTOES

This is an old fashioned sweet which requires little effort to make. You need to drop a teaspoonful of mixture into each small (preferably waxed) paper case and leave to set.

2 tbsps golden syrup

A knob of butter (or 2 tsps)

1 tbsp sugar

4 tbsps dried milk

1½ tsps peppermint essence

"Boil the syrup, butter and sugar for 2 to 3 minutes. Then remove from the heat and add the dried milk and peppermint essence."

PEPPERMINT CREAMS

There's no need to cook these. If you can resist, they are best left to chill for 24 hours so they can dry out.

1 lb icing sugar
1 white of egg (whipped until stiff)
Juice of ½ lemon
1 tsp peppermint essence

"Mix together all of the ingredients. Roll out and chill. Cut into rounds and they are ready for use."

PINEAPPLE FUDGE
Nellie Abson

Fudge is easy to make and no cooking is required. For this recipe, I use Pineapple in natural juice as the recipe adds sugar anyway. Slightly warm the juice to dissolve the gelatine in lukewarm water or simmer in a bowl over a pan of hot water.

1 large tin of pineapple
6 tbsps sugar
3 eggs
½ pint evaporated milk
1 pkt gelatine
1 lemon

"Cut the pineapple into cubes. Dissolve the gelatine in the pineapple juice. Separate the yolks of the eggs from the whites. Beat the lemon juice, sugar and yolks and add the pineapple. Whip the evaporated milk and add to the mixture. Lastly, whisk the whites until stiff and add to the mixture. Put in a greased 7 inch tin. Mark into squares when almost set. When set, cut along the marked lines."

TOFFEE:

Here are several recipes for toffee. Nowadays, you can use a temperature gauge to prevent the mixture from overheating. Most of Grandma's recipes would need to heat to 130°C (270°F). Remember my earlier advice at the beginning of this section about safety with pans when making toffee with children.

CARAMEL TOFFEE

You can use lumps or cubes of sugar. Be careful not to add the cream when the mixture is boiling too hard otherwise it will curdle.

1 teacupful of lump sugar

¼ pt water

2 tbsps golden syrup

Piece of butter – size of an egg

Flavour with vanilla essence

2 tbsps thick cream

"Put the sugar and the water in a pan and heat gently until the sugar has dissolved. Add the golden syrup, butter and vanilla essence. Boil for ½ hour in a pan until almost set. Add the cream just before the mixture sets."

RUSSIAN TOFFEE

Grandma's trick when making toffee was to use a heavy based pan to prevent the mixture from burning.

3 oz butter

1 tbsp treacle

1 teacupful sugar

1 tin evaporated milk

"Melt the butter in a pan. Add the treacle and sugar and boil up. Then add the evaporated milk and boil for 20 minutes. Stir very well. Put into a greased baking tray. When done, cut into small squares."

TOFFEE

This is the simplest toffee recipe. Grandma would boil this one slowly so the syrup didn't burn.

$\frac{1}{2}$ teacup cold water

$\frac{1}{4}$ lb butter

$\frac{1}{2}$ lb soft white sugar

$1\frac{1}{2}$ tbsps golden syrup

Juice $\frac{1}{2}$ lemon

"Put the water in the pan and add the other ingredients. Boil until set – about $\frac{1}{2}$ hour. Put into a greased baking tray and leave to set."

TREACLE TOFFEE

This is the Bonfire Night favourite. Grandma used black treacle to make it dark.

2 oz margarine

1 cup of treacle

1 lb demerara sugar

Pinch of bicarbonate of soda

1 tsp vinegar

"Melt the margarine, treacle and sugar in a pan. Add the bicarbonate of soda and beat together for 10 minutes, stirring constantly. Add the vinegar. Then pour into a buttered tin to set and cut into squares."

——V – Puddings, Pastry and Desserts ——

Grandma's pastry was the best I have ever eaten. Her apple pies were a real indulgence. For covered fruit pies, she always brushed milk on top and then sprinkled sugar on the top before putting in the oven. This ensured a crisp golden topping which everyone loved. She would always say that you needed to have 'cool' hands to make good pastry. Nowadays, we can use food mixers to make good pastry. I'm proud of the fact that I can replicate her pastry, particularly when I won first prize for an apple and blackberry pie in my local Gardeners' Association show. A number of the pudding recipes are steamed for several hours but nowadays we can do this in microwave ovens if you follow the manufacturer's instructions.

Many traditional steamed puddings also contain suet which gives them a light texture. Suet is cooking fat made from beef or mutton fat around the loins and kidneys. You can buy it shredded ready to use and there are vegetarian alternatives available.

We were a family steeped in railway history. Grandma's father (Thomas Cave), husband (William Lionel Abson who died in 1935), and son (Frederick Abson) all worked on the railway in various jobs, ranging from platelayer (my great grandfather) to station master (my father). So it is no surprise that one of the favourite family puddings is Railway Pudding!

Puddings also came in seasons – lemon puddings of all types, including Lemon Meringue Pie, were produced at the height of summer, and Plum Puddings were made in late October according to her sister Emma Tooth's recipe to mature for Christmas. My favourite is Treacle Pudding for which she won 5 shillings (25p) when it was printed in the 'South Yorkshire Times'. Some of the recipes allude to shortages during the two world wars she lived through, including the aptly named Wartime Pudding.

I have included in this section her Yorkshire Pudding recipe at which she excelled. Her trick was to make sure the fat was sizzling in the tin before putting in the mixture. We always ate them every Sunday as a starter, before the main course, often served with Raspberry Vinegar.

Contents

Grandma the competition winner.
Here she won 5s (5s shillings) for her
Treacle Pudding

Bake in a moderate oven for abou half an hour, or until brown.

* * *

Another prize of 5s. goes to **E. Abson**, **6, Station road, Bolton-on-Dearne.**

Treacle Pudding

Ingredients: One lb flour, ½lb suet, ½lb treacle, one egg, one teaspoonful ginger, one teaspoonful baking powder, one tablespoonful sugar, ½ gill milk and a pinch of salt.

Mix all the dry ingredients. Beat the egg well, add to milk and treacle, and mix all together.

Put in a greased mould and stea for two and a half hours. Serve w custard.

HOT PUDDINGS:

APPLE CHARLOTTE

I like to add blackberries to this recipe, freshly picked during the blackberrying season in early Autumn.

1 lb apples
4 oz breadcrumbs
2 oz suet
1 oz sugar
Pinch of cinnamon

"Slice the apples and place in a greased baking dish. Mix together the breadcrumbs, suet, sugar and cinnamon. Spread on top of the apples. Bake for 45 minutes until a golden brown. Serve with custard." (350°F, Mark 4, 180°C)

APPLE PIE

I'm keeping up Grandma's tradition of mouth watering pastry. Brushing the lid with a dash of milk and sprinkling a tiny bit of sugar really makes for a crisp finish. It's magical!

¹⁄₂ lb shortcrust pastry
(see V Puddings, Pastry and Desserts page 101)
1 lb apples (peeled, cored and sliced)
Lemon juice
1 tbsp sugar

"Line a pie dish or plate with pastry. Stew the apples in a pan with 1 tbsp sugar and a little lemon juice (to avoid them going brown). When the apples have fallen, spread them over the pastry in the pie dish. Roll out the pastry for the lid to cover the apples. Make a pattern round the edge of the dish with end of spoon. Brush the top of the pastry with a little milk and sprinkle sugar on top. This gives a golden crisp effect to the top. Bake in a fairly hot oven for 25 minutes. Serve with custard or cream." (400°F, Mark 6, 200°C)

APPLE AND MINCEMEAT PIE

As Apple Pie, but substitute 2 to 3 tbsps of mincemeat for some of the apple. See VII Chutneys, Pickles Jams and Jellies page 120 for Mincemeat recipe.

APPLE/MINCEMEAT or JAM LATTICE PIE

As Apple Pie, but instead of covering with lid, cut strips of pastry and twist these across the filling. This could be used to make a Jam Tart, using jam instead of the apples and mincemeat.

BAKEWELL PUDDING

There are lots of secret recipes for the real Bakewell Pudding. Grandma's recipe may not be the 'one' but it works well. I've tried adding a few ground almonds to the pastry as well for extra texture and taste.

¹/₂ lb shortcrust pastry
See V Puddings, Pastry and Desserts page 101
Raspberry jam
See VII Chutneys, Pickles Jams and Jellies page 121

Filling:
1 cupful plain flour
1 dsp baking powder
¹/₂ cupful ground almonds
4 tbsps sugar
2 eggs (beaten)
A little butter (melted)
Flaked almonds

"Line a tin with a layer of pastry. Spread with raspberry jam. Mix together the flour, baking powder, ground almonds, sugar and eggs. Melt the butter and add this to the mixture. Put on top of the jam and sprinkle flaked almonds on the top. Bake in a fairly hot oven for 20 minutes and reduce for a further 10 minutes." (400°F, Mark 6, 200°C to 350°F, Mark 4, 180°C)

BOILED LEMON PUDDING

Instead of following Grandma's recipe to make a large one, you can divide the mixture into smaller individual basins and microwave. If you use silicone moulds or bun cases, you have to put them in a conventional oven. Please check carefully.

¹/₄ lb chopped suet
¹/₂ lb breadcrumbs
3 oz moist sugar
2 oz self raising flour
1 lemon – grated rind and juice
1 egg
Milk

"Mix the suet, breadcrumbs, sugar and flour well together, adding the grated rind and strained juice of the lemon. When all the ingredients are well mixed, add the egg and sufficient milk to make a thick batter. Put into a greased basin and boil for 3 hours. Serve with sugar sprinkled over custard." See VI Sauces, Icings and Fillings page 107.

Making a perfect Apple pie

Peel and core the apples

Stew the apples

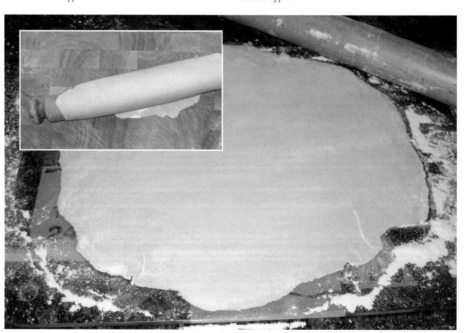

Roll out the pastry and wrap around the rolling pin

Trim the edges and make a pattern around the edge of the pie

Melt in the mouth Apple Pie ready to serve

BREAD PUDDING

'Waste not, want not' was Grandma's mantra and she made Bread Pudding with breadcrumbs to use up almost any sort of older bread. You can use whole slices of bread if you prefer.

Same quantity of breadcrumbs and raisins (e.g. 4 oz)

2 eggs (beaten)

2 oz sugar

1 pint milk

"Butter a pie dish. Use the same quantity of breadcrumbs and raisins. Mix all together. Boil up the milk. Make a custard with the eggs, milk and sugar. Pour over the rest. Bake in a moderate oven for 1½ - 2 hours." (350°F, Mark 4, 180°C)

CHOCOLATE PUDDING

In the 19th century, people used to buy sugar in conical solid blocks called loaves, hence the names of mountains such as Sugar Loaf Mountain. These would have been roughly crushed for this recipe rather than granulated. You can get the same effect by crushing sugar lumps. Together with the ground almonds, the mixture will be crunchy rather than smooth but still scrumptious.

4 oz butter

¼ lb lump sugar (crushed)

6 oz chocolate (grated)

1 oz almonds (chopped fine)

A little vanilla

4 – 5 eggs separated

"Firstly, beat the butter to a cream and then add the sugar and stir it a little. Then add the chocolate, almonds, vanilla and yolks of each egg separately. Stir the mixture for 20 minutes. Beat the whites to a froth and mix into the rest slowly. Grease the mould or basin with butter. Steam for 2 hours. It can be alternatively baked in the oven for ¾ hour." (350°F, Mark 4, 180°C)

CHOCOLATE SOUFFLE

Using breadcrumbs rather than flour gives a thicker texture to this recipe.

½ pt milk

2 oz sugar

1 oz grated chocolate

¼ lb breadcrumbs

Knob of butter

2 eggs separated

"Boil the milk, sugar and chocolate together. Add the breadcrumbs and butter. Let it stand in a warm place for a few minutes. When the mixture is cool, add the yolks. Then stir in lightly the whites of the eggs whipped to a stiff froth. Pour the mixture in to a buttered dish and bake for 35 minutes until firm to the touch." (400°F, Mark 6, 200°C)

COCONUT TART

You can also spread jam into the pastry before adding the coconut mixture if you wish. Dust the top with icing sugar once it's out of the oven for a splendid finish.

4 oz shortcrust pastry

2 oz butter

2 eggs

2 dsps sugar

A little milk

½ lb desiccated coconut

1 tsp baking powder

"Melt the butter and mix with the eggs, sugar and milk. Beat well and add the coconut and baking powder. Line a tart tin with good pastry and pour in the mixture. Bake until nicely browned for 25 minutes in a fairly hot oven." (400°F, Mark 6, 200°C)

CUP PUDDING

This is a good recipe for individual puddings.

½ lb plain flour

4 oz sugar

Grated rind of 1 lemon

1 tsp baking powder

Pinch of salt

1 egg

Milk to mix

1 oz butter to grease the cups

"Mix the flour, baking powder, sugar, lemon rind and salt together with the butter and add the well beaten egg and sufficient milk to make a stiff batter. Half fill some greased cups. Cover with greased paper and tie on. Steam for 1-1¼ hours. Turn out and serve with jam or lemon sauce."
See VI Sauces, Icings and Fillings page 108.

Clara's recipe book with precise instructions for German Pudding

GERMAN PUDDING
Clara Cave

Clara, Grandma's sister who worked in Didsbury in Manchester as a cook, always left very specific instructions in her recipes. If you don't have a cinnamon pipe as described in this recipe, try using a level teaspoonful of cinnamon powder instead. This is a light pudding.

A small pipe of cinnamon

1 gill (¼ pint) milk

2 oz butter

3 oz plain flour

3 oz caster sugar

5 eggs separated

A little grated lemon rind

Breadcrumbs

"Boil the milk with the cinnamon and butter. Stir the flour in until the mixture is quite smooth. Leave to cool. The yolks of the eggs must be then stirred with the sugar. Add the lemon rind and when well stirred put it into the rest and stir it all together. The whites of the eggs must be beaten to a froth and added slowly to the rest. The mould must be prepared with breadcrumbs and butter. Pour the mixture into the mould and then the pudding should be steamed for ½ hour. When taken out let it cool slightly before taking the cover off."

GINGER PUDDING

GROUND RICE PUDDING

This is one of my favourites. I loved to eat this pudding especially served with Almond Cream Sauce. See VI Sauces, Icings and Fillings page 107.

2 oz suet
4 oz plain flour
1 tsp baking powder
1 tsp ginger
2 oz sugar
Pinch of salt
2 oz golden syrup
1 egg (beaten)
Milk to mix

"Shred the suet very finely and mix it with the flour, baking powder, ginger, sugar and salt. Make a well in the centre and add the syrup and beaten egg. Add enough milk to make the mixture soft. Cover with a cloth and steam for 1½ hours."

We had this regularly. A special treat was to have a spoonful of homemade raspberry jam in the centre of your dish – which you swirled around to make a pattern.

1 pint boiled milk
4 tbsps plain flour or ground rice
A little butter
Pinch of salt
Sugar
Vanilla essence
Egg

"Pour the milk on the flour and beat well with a little butter. Add a pinch of salt, sugar and vanilla with a well beaten egg. Bake in a buttered dish in a moderate oven for 1 hour."
(350°F, Mark 4, 180°C)

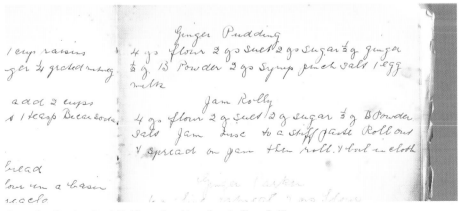

Extract from Grandma Abson's Pudding section with my favourite Ginger Pudding

JAM ROLY POLY

This is perhaps the most loved of all steamed puddings - another of those childhood favourites and really warming and comforting on a cold day.

4 oz plain flour

2 oz suet

2 oz sugar

1 tsp baking powder

Pinch of salt

Water to mix

Jam

"Mix the flour, suet, sugar, baking powder and salt with water to a stiff paste. Roll out. Spread with jam. Roll up and place in greased paper or cloth and steam for 2 hours."

KISS ME QUICK PUDDING

I can't find the origins of this pudding but it works out well and the name of it always makes people laugh. It's good to serve with homemade custard. See VI Sauces, Icings and Fillings page 107.

2 oz crushed lump sugar

¼ lb butter

2 eggs

½ lb plain flour

½ tsp bicarbonate of soda

4 tbsps Strawberry or Raspberry jam

"Beat the sugar and butter together. Add the eggs (well beaten) and flour and bicarbonate of soda. Grease a basin and put the jam in the bottom. Cover with the mixture. Cover and steam for 2 hours. Turn out."

LEMON DELICIOUS PUDDING

This Lemon Pudding is possibly my favourite. I like the way the mixture separates out into a curd at the base and a sponge on the top.

4 oz caster sugar

1½ oz butter

1½ oz plain flour

1 lemon – juice and rind

¼ pint (150ml) milk

2 eggs separated

"Cream the sugar and butter.
Add the flour, lemon juice and rind.
Beat the egg yolks in the milk and
add to the rest of the mixture.
Beat the egg whites and fold in with
a metal spoon. Bake in a greased
1½ pint pie dish for 35–45 minutes."
(350°F, Mark 4, 180°C)

LEMON MERINGUE PIE

This is an all time favourite. Grandma would make 2 or 3 at a time as it's also delicious to eat cold. I love it when the mixture is still hot and a bit runny and the meringue is freshly peaked from the oven.

8 oz shortcrust pastry

2 lemons (rind and juice)

7 oz sugar

5 tsps cornflour

2 eggs (separated)

½ pint water

"Line a dish with pastry and bake
it blind for 10–12 minutes. Put the
lemon rind and juice, 4 oz sugar and
water in a pan and heat until the
sugar is dissolved. Mix the cornflour
to a paste with 6 tbsps of water and
stir into the rest of the water until
blended. Let it cool a little then add
the egg yolks. Pour into a pastry case.
Whisk the whites of the eggs until stiff
and whisk in the rest of the sugar, a
little at a time. Spoon the meringue
onto the filling and make swirls.
Cook in a slow oven for 30 minutes."
(300°F, Mark 2 150°C)

Bake it blind

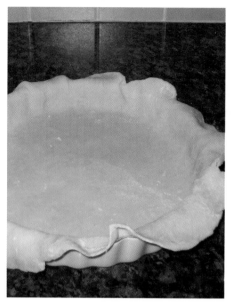

Line the flan base

Trim the edges

Insert the baking paper and pour in the dried peas or beans

Lemon Meringue Pie with a swirling topping of crisp meringue

Bakewell Pudding decorated with almond flakes

LEMON TART

This is an easy version of a lemon tart. Grandma also made this with cream rather than water which makes a richer version.

¹/₂ lb shortcrust pastry

2 tbsps cornflour

Water

1 lemon

1 egg beaten

¹/₂ cup sugar

Piece of lard/butter size of a walnut
"Line a dish or tin with pastry and bake it blind. Mix 2 tbsps of cornflour into a paste with a little cold water. Then add a cupful of boiling water. Stir until it is clear and then grate the rind of the lemon into the mixture. Add the egg, the sugar, the juice of the lemon and the lard or butter. Cook all well in a pan and spread thickly on the cooked pastry."

PANCAKES

A fool proof recipe for Pancake day. See VIII Wines, Tonics and Remedies for Raspberry Vinegar on page 126.

4 oz plain flour

Pinch of salt

2 large or 3 medium eggs

¹/₂ pint milk

Fat/oil for frying

"Mix the flour and salt in a bowl. Make a well in the centre and break in the eggs. Add ¹/₂ of the milk and beat until it is a smooth batter. Add the rest gradually and beat until well mixed. Heat the fat/oil in the frying pan until hot – pour enough of the batter in to cover the base of the pan. Cook each side in turn. Serve with Raspberry vinegar or orange juice and sugar."

PLUM PUDDING

Emma Tooth

Grandma generally made her own Plum Puddings (Christmas Pudding) a few weeks before Christmas and tied them up with clean cloth such as muslin or cotton in white basins. This recipe is from her sister Emma and was the one she used every time. Ground almonds or crushed almonds can be used for 'sweet almonds or nibs'.

2 lb currants

1 lb sultanas

1 lb stoned raisins

$\frac{1}{2}$ lb mixed peel

1 lb suet

1 lb breadcrumbs

1 lb self raising flour

1 lb (soft brown) sugar

$\frac{1}{4}$ lb sweet almonds or nibs

2 tsps mixed spice

1 tsp salt

6 eggs (beaten)

1 bottle stout

A little milk

"Mix all of the dry ingredients. Add the eggs, then the stout and milk. Mix all well. Cover with greaseproof paper. Steam or boil for 4 hours. This quantity makes 3 large puddings."

STEWART PUDDING

A majestic steamed pudding recipe with fruit. No need for weighing scales with this one. It's lovely to eat with homemade custard. See VI Sauces, Icings and Fillings on page 107.

5 tbsps plain flour

4 tbsps suet (finely chopped)

4 tbsps sugar

4 tbsps raisins

1 tsp baking powder

Pinch of salt

Milk to mix

A few sultanas

"Mix the whole together to make a stiff batter. Grease a pudding basin well, drop in a few sultanas and pour in the mixture. Steam for $2\frac{1}{2}$ hours."

RAILWAY PUDDING

I'm not sure of the origins of this, but for a railway family it had to be a favourite! The tin would be a Swiss Roll type tin – large, deep and oblong. See page 107 for custard.

1 cupful plain flour
2 tsps baking powder
1 small cupful sugar
2 eggs beaten
¾ cupful milk
Raspberry jam

"Mix the flour, baking powder and sugar together. Beat the eggs with the milk. Mix all well together. Put in a greased Yorkshire Pudding tin and bake in a quick oven for 20 minutes. (375°F, Mark 5, 190°C). When it's done, spread the jam over it and roll it up like a Swiss Roll. Serve with custard, cream or milk. It is nice eaten hot or cold."

A pudding for a railway family

Recipe for Railway Pudding

1 Cupful of Flour.
1 Small " " Sugar
2 teaspoonful Baking Powder
2 egg's beaten well with ¾ Cup of milk, mix well together. put in a greased Yorkshire pudding tin & Bake in a quick oven. when done spread jam over & roll up. & serve with either custard Sauce. Cream or milk it is nice eaten Hot or cold.

TAPIOCA CREAM

This brings back another of those childhood memories. You either loved Tapioca or hated it! The way Grandma made it with whisking the egg whites meant that it had a light texture unlike the heavy tapioca puddings we had for school dinners in the 1950s.

3 tbsps tapioca
Water
3 oz sugar
2 eggs
1 quart (2 pints) (1200ml) milk

"Cover the tapioca with water and leave it overnight. Beat 2 oz sugar with the yolks of the eggs and the tapioca (drained). Boil the milk and when boiling, pour the tapioca into the pan. Let it gently boil for 10 minutes, still stirring. Then pour into a buttered dish. Whisk the whites of the eggs with 1 oz of the sugar and fold into the mixture. Bake for 1 - 1½ hours in a slow oven."
(325°F, Mark 3, 170°C)

TREACLE PUDDING

This is a prizewinning recipe. Grandma won 5s for this recipe when it was printed in the local paper. When you turn this pudding out of the basin, the treacle mixture turns into a gorgeously gooey topping. See VI Sauces, Icings and Fillings for the recipe for custard on page 107.

1 lb plain flour
¼ lb suet
1 tsp ginger
1 tsp baking powder
1 tbsp sugar
A pinch of salt
1 egg
½ lb treacle
½ gill (⅛ pint) milk

"Mix all of the dry ingredients. Beat the egg well, add to milk and treacle and mix all together. Put in a greased basin and steam for 2½ hours. Serve with custard."

WARTIME PUDDING

In times of shortage, people had to look around to make good use of whatever they had available. This steamed pudding mixture can be used with a variety of toppings of whatever fruit is seasonal.

1 cup plain flour

2 oz fat (lard/butter)

1 tsp baking powder

1 tsp bicarbonate of soda

Milk to mix

Jam or stewed apples

"Rub the fat into the flour, baking powder and bicarbonate of soda. Add enough milk to make a soft mixture. Grease a basin and put jam or apples at the bottom. Cover with the mixture. Steam for 1 – 1½ hours. Serve with custard." See VI Sauces, Icings and Fillings page 107.

YORKSHIRE PUDDING

Yorkshire Pudding is not really a pudding but can be served as a starter to a roast or an accompaniment to a roast (usually beef). The secret tip is to get the fat really sizzling in the tin and the oven very hot. The batter should be fairly runny. I use about 4½ oz/125g flour and ½ pint/275ml milk. I find that my 'fan oven' stops Yorkshire Puddings from rising, so I switch it to a conventional heat setting to ensure they come out light and airy. Grandma usually served this with gravy and Raspberry Vinegar. See VIII Wines, Tonics and Remedies page 126.

5 tbsps plain flour (sieved and heaped)

2 eggs

Milk to mix

Salt

Fat for cooking

"Mix the ingredients to the consistency of cream. Let it stand and stir occasionally. Lift a tablespoonful of the mixture to get air in. Heat the fat in Yorkshire Pudding tins in a very hot oven. Pour in enough mixture to cover each base. Cook in the oven for 10 – 15 minutes."
(425°F, Mark 7, 220°C).

PASTRY:

Grandma made excellent pastry. It was always light and mouth-watering. She always said you needed cool hands. You can use a food mixer if your hands are warm but don't beat it for too long. She did sometimes vary the type of flour by using half quantities of plain and self raising flour to achieve a softer texture. Once you've rolled the pastry out, and put a lid of pastry on your pie, the final tip is to brush milk on the top and then sprinkle sugar on it before putting in the oven. This ensures a crisp golden topping.

SHORTCRUST PASTRY FOR GENERAL USE

2 lb plain flour

1 lb lard or lard/butter

Salt

3 tsps baking powder

Water to mix

"Rub the fat into flour, salt and baking powder. Add enough water to make a stiff dough. Leave to chill for $\frac{1}{2}$ hour before using."

SPECIAL SHORT CRUST PASTRY

7 oz lard or lard/butter

4 tbsps water

9 oz plain flour

$1\frac{1}{2}$ oz cornflour

$\frac{1}{2}$ tsp baking powder

Pinch of salt

"Heat the water and lard/butter together in a fairly large pan until the fat is completely melted. Sift the flour, cornflour, baking powder and salt into the liquid. Stir well to form a soft dough. Wrap the dough in a piece of greaseproof paper or foil and leave in a cool place or refrigerator overnight. Good for mince pies – takes $\frac{1}{2}$ lb mincemeat."

SHORTCRUST PASTRY WITH EGG

8 oz fat (lard & butter)

1 lb plain flour

Salt

1 egg

Water (or a little milk & water)

"Rub the fat into the flour and salt. When the mixture is like breadcrumbs, make a well and add the egg. Knead and add the water to make a dough. Let it stand for $\frac{1}{2}$ hour before rolling out."

DESSERTS:

COFFEE DELIGHT

Tapioca doesn't have a good press nowadays but this recipe is one of those comfort foods which conjure up happy memories of childhood. It's really easy to make.

2 pints milk
2 tbsps coffee
(essence or powdered instant)
4 tsps pearl tapioca
2 tbsps sugar
Vanilla essence
Marshmallows to decorate

"Boil the milk and add the coffee. Sprinkle the tapioca and stir until cooked. Add the sugar and vanilla essence. Leave until cold when it should be thick and creamy before turning into glasses. Decorate with marshmallows."

DAFFODIL CREAM
Nellie Abson

This was served as a special treat when people came to tea. It is another recipe from Nellie, Grandma's daughter-in-law. We had a spread of cold ham and salad followed by this scrumptiously fluffy and airy dessert. I've made it with fresh pineapple as an alternative to tinned.

$\frac{1}{2}$ oz gelatine
1 tin pineapple in natural juice
6 oz sugar
3 eggs
Grated rind and juice of 1 lemon
$\frac{1}{2}$ pint evaporated milk

"Dissolve the gelatine in the juice from the tin of pineapple. Cut the pineapple finely and add to the sugar and yolks of eggs. Then add the lemon juice, grated rind and the pineapple juice. Whip the $\frac{1}{2}$ pint evaporated milk to a froth and whip the egg whites stiffly. Leave to set in a cool place."

LEMON DESSERT

This is a pleasant tea time treat which nowadays you can serve with a fruit salad. She would serve up this dish with tinned fruit cocktail. We are fortunate to have access to exotic fruits which weren't around in Grandma's time.

1 oz gelatine
1 pint water
1 lb sifted sugar
Juice of 4 lemons
Whites of 4 eggs

"Dissolve the gelatine in 1 pint of water. Put the sugar into a large basin. Add the lemon juice and the gelatine with the water when lukewarm. Whisk the whites of the eggs until a stiff froth and add to the rest. Whisk the whole until stiff. Put into a wet mould (not a tin one)."

LEMON JELLY DELIGHT

Jellies are easy to make and always loved by children. This one has cream added. 1 gill is about ¼ pint or 150ml.

½ oz gelatine
1 gill water
3 lemons
½ lb lump sugar
3 eggs
1 gill cream

"Dissolve the gelatine in boiling water. Squeeze the juice of 1 lemon over the sugar. Beat the eggs with the sugar and add the grated rind of 3 lemons. Add a gill of cream and the dissolved gelatine and water when cool. Strain through a coarse muslin cloth into a mould."

ORANGE CREAM

This is a very pleasant cold dessert which can be served with fruit salad. It also makes a good accompaniment to Orange Cake, instead of a filling. See I Cakes on page 43.

6 large oranges

1 lemon

6 oz isinglass or gelatine

Sugar to taste

Water

½ pint cream

"Squeeze the juice from the oranges and lemon. Strain it and put into a saucepan with the isinglass or gelatine and sufficient water to make the whole 1½ pints. Rub the sugar on the orange and lemon rind. Add the rind to the mixture. Boil for 10 minutes and then strain through a sieve. Leave to cool. When cold, beat up with the cream. Soak the mould well in water, pour in the mixture and put in a cool place to set."

RHUBARB MOULD

Grandma stewed rhubarb with a little water, but I've also discovered that you can cook the chopped pieces in the oven at 375F, Mark 5, 190C for about 20 minutes with a little brown sugar sprinkled on top. This works just as well.

1 oz gelatine to each pound
of rhubarb

Sugar to taste

"Stew the rhubarb in the ordinary way. Add the gelatine when the fruit is cooked. Pour into a wetted mould until set. Any other fruit such as prunes, figs or dates can be used instead of rhubarb."

SNOW CREAM

This is another recipe which brings back childhood memories. You could serve it with fruit but we used to have a spoonful of homemade raspberry or strawberry jam. See VII Chutney, Pickles and Jams on page 121.

4 oz ground rice

2 oz loaf sugar

2 oz butter

A little almond flavouring

1 quart (2 pints) milk

"Boil the ground rice, sugar, butter and almond flavouring for 15 minutes in the milk until it is a smooth substance, though not too thick. Then pour into a mould, which has been dipped into cold water. Serve when cold with a little preserve."

STRAWBERRY AMBROSIA

This is a pleasant summer recipe to try when there is a glut of strawberries. To make the custard, see VI Sauces, Icings and Fillings page 107.

³/₄ lb strawberries

2 tbsps lemon juice

1 tsp gelatine

1-2 oz sugar

¹/₄ pt custard

¹/₄ pt cream

"Cream the strawberries, leaving a few whole for decoration. Dissolve the gelatine in lemon juice. Add the sugar and put the liquid into the strawberries. Fold in the cold custard. Put into glasses and leave to stiffen. Decorate with fruit."

VI – Sauces, Icings and Fillings

Grandma didn't just serve up custard with puddings. Almond Cream Sauce adds an extra dimension to the taste of the sponge puddings in the previous section. She always served this with her Ginger Pudding. The Custard recipe turns out really thick and creamy. I still make Rum Sauce like Grandma at Christmas to serve with the Christmas Pudding.

The icings and fillings are used to decorate the cakes and buns once they are cool.

Almond Paste is used to decorate the top of the Christmas Cake before the sugar icing or other decoration with nuts and dried fruit. To ice a cake, such as Christmas Cake or Bride's Cake, you need to let the cake be thoroughly cold and mature before covering with the Almond Paste. Then, make sure it is firm before decorating with the Sugar Icing. I usually decorate my Christmas Cakes with nuts, glace cherries and dried fruit such as raisins and glaze them with a mixture of warmed apricot jam and redcurrant jelly. See I Cakes on pages 22 and 23.

Contents

SAUCES:

ALMOND CREAM SAUCE
Clara Cave

Grandma served this sauce with steamed puddings such as German, Ginger or Treacle Puddings. See V Puddings, Pastries and Desserts on pages 90, 91 and 99.

6 blanched almonds

4 oz sugar

1 tbsp orange water

1 gill (¼ pint) cream

2 eggs (yolks only)

"Scald the almonds and put them in a mortar with the sugar and orange water. Bruise them into a pulp and then put them into a pan. Add the cream and the yolk of the eggs. With a wire whisk, whip the sauce over a very slow heat until it becomes a substantial froth. This sauce is for puddings."

CUSTARD

This can be served as a hot sauce with Jam Roly Poly, Kiss Me Quick or Stewart Pudding. See V Puddings, Pastries and Desserts on pages 92 and 97. Grandma would also flavour custard with cinnamon, nutmeg or lemon rind. If you cook it over a gentle heat, it will allow the custard to set.

1 basinful of creamy milk

4 eggs (yolks only)

Loaf sugar to sweeten

2 bay leaves to flavour

Rum if desired

"Put the milk and eggs in a pan over heat, but don't let it boil. Add the sugar to taste and bay leaves. Put a little rum in after taking the custard from the heat. Remove the bay leaves before use."

LEMON OR ORANGE SAUCE

This is good to serve with several of the steamed puddings including 'Cup Pudding'. See V Puddings, Pastries and Desserts on page 90.

Grated rind and juice of 2 lemons
(or 2 oranges)
3 tbsps sugar
2 tbsps cornflour
1 pint water

"Add the lemon or orange rind and juice to the water. Blend the cornflour and sugar with a little of the water and beat to a smooth cream. Heat the water and add the blended cornflour mixture, stirring all the time. Bring to the boil and continue stirring until the sauce is thick and clear. You can add an egg yolk at the end."

RUM SAUCE

We always serve this every year with Christmas Pudding. A family favourite.

2 oz cornflour
1 pt milk
2 tbsps golden syrup
Rum (to taste)

"Blend the cornflour with a little of the milk. Add the rest of the milk and the golden syrup. Stir continuously until boiled. Cool for a few minutes, and then add the rum. Serve with Plum Pudding." See V Puddings, Pastries and Desserts on page 97.

ICINGS:

ALMOND PASTE

These recipes are all essential to decorate Celebration Fruit Cakes. See I Cakes on pages 21, 22 and 23. You need to firstly cover the Fruit Cake with a layer of Almond Paste (or marzipan). It's a good idea to spread a thin layer of Apricot Jam over the cake before placing the layer of rolled out Almond Paste on the top and sides. Grandma always made her own Almond Paste (or marzipan).

You can also just use a few tablespoonfuls of water and/or lemon juice and omit the egg if you wish. Grandma also sometimes used to add a little sherry or brandy to the mixture. The Mock Almond Paste recipe is a wartime one when ground almonds were in short supply.

½ lb ground almonds

¾ lb caster sugar

1 egg (beaten)

"Mix the almonds and sugar together. Add sufficient egg to make a stiff paste. One egg may be enough for a small cake."

MOCK ALMOND PASTE

4 oz margarine

2 tbsps water

2 tsps almond essence

4 oz sugar

4 oz soya flour

A little egg

"Melt the margarine in the water. Move from the heat and add 2 tsps of almond essence. Stir in the sugar and soya flour and knead well. A little egg if added improves this".

CHOCOLATE ICING

*This can be used for icing a Chocolate Cake.
See I Cakes page 25.*

3 oz chocolate

4 oz icing sugar

Water

"Place the chocolate in a saucepan to
melt. Add the icing sugar and enough
cold water to moisten it. Let it boil
quickly for 10 minutes."

SUGAR ICING

*The Sugar Icing goes on top of the Almond
Paste. If decorating a Christmas Cake isn't
your forte, you can always use a fork to make
peaks in the icing to simulate a snow scene.*

1 lb icing sugar

$1\frac{1}{2}$ whites of eggs

A little lemon juice

"Sift sugar and add a little lemon
juice and enough whites of the eggs to
make it like whipped cream. Beat for
15 minutes or until it will adhere to
the spoon when held up. Do not beat
too long. It may be necessary to add a
little more sugar."

FILLINGS:

BUTTER CREAM

Use this to join the 2 layers of a Victoria Sandwich. See I Cakes page 47.

2 oz butter
4 oz icing sugar
Few drops vanilla essence
1-2 tbsps tepid water or milk

"Cream the butter and icing sugar. Add the vanilla essence and water or milk."

ORANGE CREAM FILLING

Grandma always used this with the Orange (Ring) Cake recipe. See I Cakes page 43.

5 oz icing sugar
2 oz butter
Juice of ½ orange

"Put all together and beat until soft."

VII – Chutneys, Pickles, Jams & Jellies

Nowadays, we are in the midst of a revival of interest in growing garden produce and these recipes show what Grandma did in her day when there was a glut of fruit and vegetables to use. Grandma relied on a regular source of produce to make a supply of chutneys and pickles to last through the winter. Green Tomato Chutney would use up tomatoes which didn't ripen before the end of the summer and the marrow recipes used up the numerous marrows which seemed to grow in plentiful supply. Grandma used a large aluminium pan with a thick wide base for chutneys. To test if the chutney was ready, she would draw a wooden spoon across the bottom of the pan. If it's ready, the chutney must not flow back into the gap left behind by the spoon. If not, then check every 5 minutes or so until the gap is clear.

Grandma used blackcurrants from the garden to make Blackcurrant Jelly and strawberries and raspberries to make jam to last throughout the winter. She had a large jam pan with a brass interior, which I still have, to make jam and jellies. She would pot the jam up into clean jam jars and place small waxed discs over the surface of the jam. Then she tied cellophane covers on the top and secured them with a rubber band or string. Don't forget to label and date the jars if you do this.

In this section, I have also included a more recent grandma, Grandma Pat White, who makes fantastic marmalade every February for all the White family.

Grandma always made sure that the jam jars for chutneys, pickles, jams and jellies were thoroughly clean by washing and rinsing them and allowing them to dry in a hot oven. Once cool, she covered them with a clean tea towel ready for use.

People still enjoy making homemade produce. Remember that homemade jams and chutneys do not keep for as long as commercial ones which contain artificial preservatives.

Contents

*Home made marmalade to
Grandma Abson's recipe*

CHUTNEYS:

APPLE CHUTNEY

Chutney needs to be allowed to cool slowly so it produces a tangy flavour. Grandma chopped the fruit and onions finely since the final consistency of the chutney should be thick and smooth. Grandma served this with pork pies at Christmas.

2 lb apples
1½ lb onions
1 lb dried apricots
1 lb sultanas
1 lb demerara sugar
2 oz garlic
1½ tbsps salt
1 tbsp ground ginger
1 quart vinegar

"Chop up the apples, onions and apricots. Add the other ingredients and mix together. Put all of the ingredients through a mincer. Place in a pan and bring to the boil. Simmer for about 1½ hours, stirring until the ingredients are tender. Spoon into jars and cover."

GREEN TOMATO CHUTNEY

This is a good recipe which will keep well over the winter. It needs to mature for a couple of months before using. Grandma served this with cold meats.

8 lb green tomatoes
4 onions
3 lb cooking apples
1 lb large stoned raisins
1 lb demerara sugar
1 oz mustard seed
4 tbsps salt
1 tsp allspice
1 tsp ground ginger
A little pepper
2 quarts vinegar

"Cut the tomatoes, apples and onions into small pieces. Add the other ingredients. Boil all ingredients together for 2½ hours. Put in jars and cover when cool."

PICKLES:

TOMATO CHUTNEY

This has a finer texture than the coarser Green Tomato Chutney. You can use muslin instead of a fine sieve.

4 lb tomatoes

1 lb cooking apples

$\frac{1}{2}$ dozen small onions

$1\frac{1}{2}$ pints vinegar

1 oz mustard seed

$\frac{1}{2}$ oz grated ginger

4 oz salt

$\frac{1}{2}$ tsp cayenne pepper

1 lb sugar (brown)

$\frac{1}{2}$ tsp allspice

10 cloves

"Skin the tomatoes. Chop the apples and the onions. Boil the vinegar and place all the other ingredients with it. Boil until soft. Put this through a coarse sieve and set aside to cool. Stir daily for 3 days. Bottle and cork tightly or put in jars."

CHOW CHOW PICKLE

The vinegar acts as the preservative. You have to make sure all the ingredients are covered with the vinegar. Grandma tended to use good quality malt vinegar to give the pickle a darker colour.

2 lbs green tomatoes

$\frac{1}{2}$ head cabbage

4 small onions

1 bundle chopped celery

1 green pepper chopped

1 tsp salt

1 tbsp mustard seed

1 tbsp celery seed

1 tsp mixed spice

$2\frac{1}{2}$ cups sugar

Vinegar to cover

"Chop up the tomatoes, cabbage and onions. Put in salt to stand overnight. Drain dry and add the celery, pepper, salt, spices and sugar. Cover with vinegar and boil for 30 minutes. Allow to cool. Spoon into jars and cover."

JAMS & JELLIES:

PICKLED MARROW

My father took delight in growing large marrows. Grandma only used the best quality marrows for pickling. She served this with cold meats.

1 marrow
Salt
Vinegar to cover
$\frac{1}{2}$ lb sugar
1 tsp turmeric
$1\frac{1}{2}$ oz mustard powder
1 tsp cayenne powder

"Peel a nice marrow and cut it up into small squares. Sprinkle with salt and allow to stand for $1\frac{1}{2}$ hours. Then strain and put into a pan. Cover with vinegar. Add the sugar, turmeric, mustard and cayenne. Boil until the marrow is tender."

APPLE JELLY

Grandma refers to a 'flannel bag'. This would be a double thickness of a fine cloth such as muslin or a fine cotton tea towel. You could also add finely chopped mint leaves to this recipe and serve it with lamb.

"Simmer 2 lb apples in 1 quart (2 pints) of water until tender. Strain through a flannel bag. Add 2 lb sugar, 1 lemon and $\frac{1}{2}$ oz gelatine. Simmer all together until it jellies."

APRICOT JAM

Tartaric acid is sometimes known as Cream of Tartar. It helps extract the natural pectin from the fruit to help it set and keep its flavour once the fruit has been boiled.

$1\frac{1}{2}$ lb dried apricots
$7\frac{1}{2}$ cups of water
$5\frac{1}{2}$ lb sugar
1 tsp tartaric acid

"Wash the apricots well and cover with the water. Let it stand for 24 hours. Boil until tender. Then add the sugar. Boil quickly for 1 hour. Before it is fully cooked, add the tartaric acid. Leave to cool and put in jars, then cover."

BLACKCURRANT JELLY

Grandma made jelly with blackcurrants so there would be no skins or seeds to get stuck in your teeth.

Blackcurrants

Water to cover

Sugar 1 lb for each pint of fruit juice

Brandy if desired

"Remove all stalks. Then cover the fruit with water. Bring to boiling point and keep simmering for 20 minutes, stirring occasionally. Strain through a piece of muslin or sieve. Return the liquid to the pan and bring to the boil. Add the sugar. Stir thoroughly until the sugar is dissolved. The jelly should thicken. A teaspoonful of brandy added helps it to keep."

LEMON CURD

Grandma made small quantities of lemon curd unless she was giving it away to friends or for Chapel Fairs. It needs to be eaten within a couple of weeks. This recipe makes about 2 lbs.

1 lb lump sugar

6 eggs

3 lemons

$1/4$ lb butter

"Mix together the sugar and eggs, leaving out the whites of 2 eggs. Add the juice of 3 lemons and grated rind of 2 lemons. Stir in the butter over a slow heat but do not let it boil. Take it off when it is about the thickness of honey. Place in jars and cover"

MARMALADE JELLY

Seville oranges make the tastiest marmalade. They are only available for a short season in January/February. This recipe makes about 6-7lbs.

6 Seville oranges

6 pints cold water

Caster sugar

"Slice 6 Seville oranges very thinly, first cutting them into quarters and picking out the seeds. To each orange add 1 pint of cold water. Let it stand for 24 hours, then boil until the chips are tender. Allow this to stand until the next day. Then measure it and to every pint of this boiled fruit, add 1 lb of caster sugar. Then boil the whole until the syrup jellies and the chips become clear. This may take 1½ hours gently boiling. The 6 oranges will make a nice quantity."

MARMALADE with THREE FRUITS

The 3 fruits give this marmalade a different flavour. You also have to cook it for longer, around 1-2 hours, so you need to use more water.

3 grapefruit

3 oranges

1 lemon

Sugar

Water

"Cut all of the fruit into shreds and put the pith and pips into a small linen bag. Cover all with water and let it stand overnight. Then boil until the shreds are tender. To every 1 lb of fruit add 1¼ lbs of sugar."

GRANDMA PAT'S ORANGE MARMALADE

Grandma Pat still makes marmalade in her eighties. She shortens the time for boiling by chopping the peel finely in a food processor and using a pressure cooker. This also requires less water.

1 lb Seville oranges
1 pint water
2 lbs sugar

"Squeeze the oranges (I use 2 lbs oranges at a time), remove the pith and pips and put them in a muslin bag. Either cut up the peel, or as I do, process it in food processor. Put the juice, bag of pips and pith and chopped peel with ½ pint of water in a pressure cooker for 10-15 minutes until the peel is soft. Remove muslin bag, add sugar and remaining water. I use a large preserving pan. Bring it all to the boil, and keep stirring. Fast boil (not simmer) for 15 minutes. Leave for about 10 minutes before potting. Makes about 6 lbs."

MARROW CURD

This is a wartime recipe, used to eke out lemons if they were in short supply.

2 lb marrow peeled and chopped
2 lb sugar
¼ lb butter
3 small or 2 large lemons

"Steam the marrow until tender. Put in a pan with lemon juice and rind, sugar and butter. Boil for 20 minutes. Excellent substitute for lemon curd."

MARROW LEMON CHEESE or MARROW CREAM

Another wartime recipe to serve instead of lemon curd.

4 lb marrow peeled and chopped
3 lb sugar
½ lb margarine
9 lemons

"Steam the marrow until tender with a little salt. Then beat to a pulp. Add the juice of the lemons and grated rind, margarine and sugar. Boil for ½ hour. This quantity makes 10 lb."

MINCEMEAT

Mince pies made with homemade mincemeat taste so much more delicious. Mincemeat is actually a mixture of dried fruits and apples. You could use vegetable suet instead of meat based suet if you are vegetarian. I usually make mincemeat about 2-3 weeks before Christmas to allow it to mature.

1 ½ lb apples
Rind and juice of 1 lemon
A little salt
A little nutmeg
A little allspice
½ lb suet
1 lb demerara sugar
1 lb stoned raisins
¾ lb currants
½ lb sultanas
¼ lb mixed peel

"Peel and cut the apples into small chunks. Add the rind and juice of the lemon, salt, nutmeg and allspice. Shred the suet and place in a stew jar in the oven until the apples are soft and the suet is melted. Then take out, stir in the sugar and other fruit. When cold, place in jars and it is ready for use."

PLUM JAM

Grandma didn't have a Plum tree in the garden but she was sometimes given plums by kindly neighbours when they had a glut. Making Plum Jam is a good way to use them up.

3 lbs plums
3 lbs sugar
½ pint water
Knob of butter

"Wash the fruit and lay out on trays. Sprinkle a little sugar on the plums and leave for an hour. Transfer the plums to the preserving pan and simmer in the water for 30 minutes until the fruit is really soft. Add the sugar and stir until it has dissolved. Add the knob of butter. Boil for about 30 minutes and test for setting. Remove the stones and scum with a spoon. Leave to cool. Then put in jars and cover."

RASPBERRY JAM

Raspberry Jam is generally one of the easiest to make since it will set reasonably well. Grandma had a set of Kilner jars which you can still get today. She would sterilise the jars in the coal oven before potting up the jam for us to relish on scones, puddings and desserts throughout the year. If you use about 3lbs of fruit, this recipe make about 5-6 lbs of jam.

Raspberries
Sugar 1 lb for each pound of fruit

"Wash and drain the fruit. Let it simmer in its own juice for about 20-30 minutes until soft. Add the sugar and stir until it has dissolved. Boil for about 30 minutes and test for setting. Remove the scum with a spoon. Leave to cool, put in jars and cover."

STRAWBERRY JAM

Grandma used to use strawberries for jam once my father started to grow them in the garden. She would probably use about 3-4 lbs of fruit at a time. This would make about 5-6 jars of jam.

Strawberries
Sugar 1 lb for each pound of fruit
1 tbsp lemon juice for each pound of fruit

"Wash and hull the fruits and place in the pan with the lemon juice. Simmer for 30 minutes until soft. Add the sugar, stirring until it has all dissolved. Boil for 20 minutes and test for setting. Remove the scum with a spoon. Leave to cool, put in jars and cover."

Grandma Abson's traditional jam pot

VII – Wines, Tonics and Remedies

You may find some of the recipes in this section amusing though they are all from Grandma's collection of recipes for medicinal purposes! They include Pick Me Up Tonic and Invalid Custard to tempt a sick member of the family back to eating. The Celebrated Wath Butterscotch comes from her days in service with the Hick Family of chemists in Wath-on-Dearne. Grandma would take advantage of the free elderberries which were in full bloom and rampant in August every year in the station yard and make copious amounts of Elderberry Syrup to ward off coughs and colds in the winter months. Raspberry Vinegar was my favourite for gargling for a sore throat and my university friends were introduced to its soothing qualities.

My friends and I have made some of these recipes : Elderflower Sparkling Wine, Elderberry Syrup and Raspberry Vinegar. I have included them all to complete the record of my Grandma's recipes.

Contents

WINES:

ELDERFLOWER SPARKLING WINE

2 pints of heads of elderflower
in full bloom

1 gallon (8 pints) cold water

1 lemon

1½ lb sugar

2 tbsp white wine vinegar

"Squeeze the juice out of the lemon.
Cut the rind into 4 pieces and put
with the elderflowers, sugar and
vinegar in a large jug. Pour on cold
water and steep for 24 hours.
Strain and bottle. Keep for 2 weeks
before corking."

ORANGE WINE

10 oranges to a gallon (8 pints)
of water

5 lb sugar

"Cut up the oranges and let them
stand in water for a fortnight.
Use the peel from 5 and put in a
warm oven until they are golden
brown. Add them to a quart of
boiling water. Strain and boil, then
add to 5 lbs of sugar. When nearly
cold, strain the rest of the liquid and
add together."

PARSLEY WINE

1 lb parsley to each gallon (8 pints)
(4.5 litres) of water

2 oranges

2 lemons

1 oz ginger

1 oz yeast

4 lb sugar

"Pour the boiling water over the
parsley and let it stand for 24 hours.
Then stir and boil with the thin peel
of the oranges and lemons. Add the
ginger and sugar and boil for ½ hour.
Peel all the white off the oranges
and the lemons. Cut the oranges and
lemons up small. Put in a bowl and
pour the wine over slowly. Allow to
cool and when just warm add the
yeast and sugar pounded up with a
little of the liquor. Let it stand for
two to three days. Strain and bottle.
Leave for two or three months before
corking up tightly."

MOCK PORT WINE

4 lbs beetroot

4 quarts of water

$\frac{1}{2}$ lb sugar

1 lemon

A few cloves

Root ginger

"Wash well and cut into pieces as quickly as possible. Put the pieces into cold water. Use 1 quart to every 1lb. Boil until tender and all colour possible extracted. Strain and to every quart of liquor, add $\frac{1}{2}$ lb sugar, the juice of one lemon, a few cloves and a piece of root ginger. Stir well until the sugar is dissolved. Cover over and leave for 2 weeks. At the end of that time, bottle but cork lightly until fermentation ceases. A little brandy added to each bottle is an improvement. If kept a year, this wine is like port."

RHUBARB WINE

$5\frac{1}{2}$ lb rhubarb

1 gallon of cold water

$\frac{1}{2}$ oz root ginger

1 lemon

$4\frac{1}{2}$ lb sugar

"Let it stand for 14 days. Then strain and bring to the boil with $\frac{1}{2}$ oz root ginger and 1 lemon to each gallon. When lukewarm, add $4\frac{1}{2}$ lb of sugar. Leave it for a week. Then strain and bottle. Do not cork up tight until it has finished working."

TONICS:

TONIC

"Cut up a beetroot and add 1 lb demerara sugar. Let it stand for 24 hours. Strain and add a bottle of stout. Good for anaemia."

DR. WHITE'S TONIC

1 bottle Port Wine

1 lb malt

2 oz Bovril

2d (= twopence or 2 old pennies = 1p) worth of quinine

"Dissolve malt in a jug in a pan of boiling water. Add the Bovril, quinine and then the wine. Bottle when cold. Dose – 1 wineglass 3 times a day."

PICK ME UP TONIC

"Wipe 4 new laid eggs. Put them in a basin and squeeze over them the juice of 3 lemons. Let the eggs be in the juice for 3 days, turning them over every day. On the fourth day, beat up the eggs, shell and all and strain them through a sieve into another basin in which put ¼ lb caster sugar dissolved in ¾ pint of new milk and ½ pint of rum. Bottle and keep in a cool place. Take a wineglassful every day. Improves with keeping. N.B. Grandma writes that she made double this quantity and it took a 12/6 (63p) bottle of rum."

WINE TONIC RECIPE

1 pint of Old Beer or Magnate Ale

½ pint of black beer

1 tsp Peruvian bark

1 tbsp brown sugar

"Bring the beer to boiling point; add black beer, sugar and Peruvian bark. Stir well. You can add ⅓ bottle of phosferine if liked. Take a wineglass three times a day."

REMEDIES:

BRONCHITIS AND ASTHMA COUGH MIXTURE

1d (= 1 old penny) oil of peppermint
1d of aniseed
1d of white wine vinegar
1d spirit of ether
$^1/_2$ lb black treacle

"Mix together. Put in a bottle
and shake well before taking.
1 tablespoonful night and day."

ELDERBERRY SYRUP

"Stew the berries in a large pan very
slowly over a low heat for the juice.
When ready, strain through a sieve or
cloth. For each pint of juice, add 1 lb
sugar. Simmer very slowly until the
sugar has dissolved. Let the syrup cool
and then bottle."

INVALID CUSTARD
Very Good Recipe

1 egg
1 tsp sugar
$^1/_4$ pint creamy milk (or single cream)

"Beat the egg and add the sugar and
milk. Pour into a greased cup and
steam for 20 minutes."

LEMON SYRUP

2 large or 3 small lemons
$1^1/_4$ lb lump sugar
1 oz citric acid
1 pint water

"Take the rind from the lemons.
Squeeze the juice and put both into
a jug with the sugar and citric acid.
Then pour upon all 1 pint of boiling
water. Stir until dissolved. When cold,
strain and bottle."

RASPBERRY VINEGAR

Raspberries
Vinegar to cover
Water
Sugar

"Place the raspberries in a bowl and
cover with vinegar. Stir from time
to time. After two days, strain them
through a muslin cloth. For each
pint of juice, add 1 lb of sugar. Boil
the juice and sugar for 15 minutes.
Then bottle it. Good when poured on
Yorkshire Pudding. Excellent for sore
throats as a gargle."

RHUBARB TONIC

"Squeeze 10 sticks of rhubarb into a bowl (like wringing cloths). Add 2 lb of sugar and 1 teaspoonful of ginger. Then pour over 4 quarts (8 pints) of boiling water. Allow to cool, then mix ½d (= an old halfpenny) of yeast with some of the liquid and stir in. Stand overnight and bottle."

THE CELEBRATED WATH BUTTERSCOTCH

This simple but excellent sweetmeat is considered an infallible remedy for coughs, colds etc, and is by many influential families considered equal if not superior to the Doncaster Royal.

½ a teacupful of water
½ lb of treacle
¾ lb of sugar
3 oz of butter

"Essence of lemon may be added, according to the taste of the invalid. Mix all together. Boil for 20 minutes, put into a greased baking tray and leave to set."

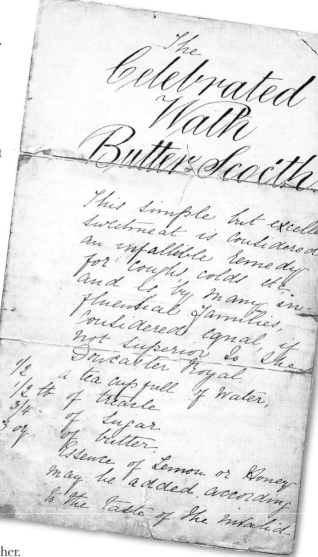

Grandma's Celebrated Wath Butterscotch recipe

My Recipes

My Recipes

My Recipes

My Recipes

My Recipes

My Recipes

My Recipes

Index

Index

Index

Index